D1560783

David Frances Barry
Icastinyanka Cikala Hanzi
(The Little Shadow Catcher)

"Icastinyanka Cikala Hanzi"
The Little Shadow Catcher

D. F. BARRY

Celebrated Photographer of Famous Indians

BY THOMAS M. HESKI

Superior PUBLISHING COMPANY

SEATTLE

Library of Congress Cataloging in Publication Data

Heski, Thomas M.—1947
The Little Shadow Catcher
Icastinyanka Cikala Hanzi

1. Barry, David F., d. 1934
2. Photographers—The West—Biography.
I. Title.
TR140.B28H47   770'.92'4 [B]   78-12579
ISBN 0-87564-808-8

FIRST EDITION

PRINTED AND BOUND IN THE UNITED STATES OF AMERICA

ACKNOWLEDGMENTS

The trail of D. F. Barry's life was a long one. I can see now why a major work on his life has never been undertaken. At times the trail was rocky and filled with ambushes. Many times I was saved by the cavalry in the form of the U.S. mail.

Periodically my wife mentioned that everything was in a disorganized state and that I'm messy! I agree. Therefore, if I have omitted anyone who has helped in my endeavor, it was not intended.

Many people have aided me directly or indirectly to try and chart out D. F. Barry's trail. I am particularly indebted to:

Alex Ladenson, The Chicago Public Library

Neal J. Ney, Chicago Historical Society

Mrs. Phillip G. Stratton

Floyd T. Ryan, Standing Rock Agency, Fort Yates, North Dakota

Michael Witkin

Mr. and Mrs. Robert Lautigar

John Kardon

Eleanor M. Gehres, Denver Public Library for information and photographs

Frank Vyzralek, North Dakota State Historical Society for information, photographs, The Hutchinson Papers and his invaluable criticism and help.

John S. Gray for a copy of his manuscript "Some Photographers of the Custer Scene".

B. William Henry Jr., Historian, Fort Laramie National Historic Site, Fort Laramie, Wyoming.

Henry W. Brown, for giving me the "Barry Bug", and his interest in D. F. Barry.

Ernest Lisle Reedstrom, artist, historian and my bunkie.

The Custer Battlefield National Monument for copies of the Elizabeth B. Custer-D.F. Barry correspondence and authoritative information.

Ken Heyer

The Little Big Horn Associates for their great help. Long may our guidon wave!

Mrs. J. W. Albmeyer, The Free Library, Quincy, Illinois.

Louis M. Nourse, St. Louis Public Library, St. Louis, Missouri.

U.S. Bureau of Census, Washington, D.C.

The original Kiwedinang Indian Dance Team, Nahak Lodge #526, Order of the Arrow, Lake Superior Council, Boy Scouts of America for help in assisting me set up the D.F. Barry Indian Collection at the Douglas County Historical Museum, Superior, Wisconsin.

Gary VanKauwenberg, for his photography skill.

Bruce R. Liddic

Dr. Milton O. Gustafson, Civil Archives Division, General Services Administration, National Archives and Records Service, Washington, D.C.

John Spence and Dorothy Malone, Honeoye Falls, Mendon Historical Society, New York.

Honeoye Falls Times

Frank A. Young, St. Louis County Historical Society, Duluth, Minnesota.

Marjorie Cox

Lloyd P. Hiatt, William S. Hart County Park, Newhall, California, for letters between W.S. Hart and D.F. Barry, information and photographs.

Superior Public Library, Superior, Wisconsin.

C. B. Costello, The Duluth Herald and News Tribune.

Don Russell

New York Historical Society

New York Public Library

Richard I. Frost, Buffalo Bill Museum, Cody, Wyoming, for information concerning W. F. Cody and D. F. Barry, and "The Barry Room".

Chet Shore

Charles Erickson, Ft. Lincoln State Park, Mandan, North Dakota.

Robert Marion Craig III, for information and his military expertise.

Rodney Paulson, for his military expertise.

Doyle Swisher for his military expertise.

Kenneth W. Rapp, archivist, United States Military Academy, West Point, New York.

Reverend Dominic Russo for information on John Martin.

Margaret Gleason, Wisconsin State Historical Society, Madison, Wisconsin.

Mrs. Lois B. Price, Portage Free Library, Portage, Wisconsin.

Elmer Olson

Norman Paulson, North Dakota Historical Society.

Harriett C. Meloy, and Nancy F. Dunnan, Montana Historical Society.

Hal Babbit, Oregon Shipbuilding Corporation.

Walter E. Oates and Victor A. Yorski, U.S. Dept. of Commerce, Maritime Administration, Washington, D.C.

Margaret C. Blaker, National Museum of Natural History, Smithsonian Institution, Washington, D.C.

Mrs. Pat Gudmundson, Miles City Star, Miles City, Montana.

Mrs. Mary Glaser, The Bismarck Tribune
Robert Scanlan
Mrs. Elmo Scott Watson
Eugene A. Burdick
Polish Embassy, Washington, D.C.
Susan Washburn, Western Publications, Inc.
The Billings Gazette
Mrs. Eunice Barry for information and permission to copy old letters and newspapers.
Mrs. Margaret Lee, Columbus Public Library, Columbus, Wisconsin.
Reverend Michael Hogan, St. Paul of the Cross Catholic Church, Honeoye Falls, New York.
Reverend Ambrose Holzer, St. Jerome's Catholic Church, Columbus, Wisconsin
Vernon and Ceil Barry for assisting me with information concerning family history, old photographs and constant help by letter. It was through these two fine beautiful people's help that many of the gaps in D.F. Barry's life fell into place. Ceil Barry was a valuable asset in the completion of this work. I thank her from the bottom of my heart.

James E. Lundsted, Curator-Director, Douglas County Historical Museum, Superior, Wisconsin, for information, photographs, and interest in my project. Mr. Lundsted's help was monumental in the completion of this work.
Bob Heski, my brother, for photographs, criticism and his aid in helping me follow the trail of Barry. Few people have a companionship as unique as the Heski brothers.
Lastly, I would like to thank my faithful partner, Linda, and our three adorable children, Christina, Thomas and Michael who have suffered much while I traveled hallowed ground. To many people, the West means California. To my family, it meant packing up and traveling to the Dakotas and Montana on a new lead.
My wife has typed, edited and criticized. I am indebted to her forever. Without her constant help, D.F. Barry's life story wouldn't have been written.

Thomas Martin Heski
February 22, 1978

EDMUND BARRY was born in 1822 in Lakes of Killarney, County Kerry, Ireland. While he was quite young, his widowed mother died and he was brought up by his eldest brother. Edmund was a shoemaker, and a farmer among other things. After his wife's death, he moved to Chicago. In 1906, he moved to St. Louis, Missouri, where he resided until his death December 10, 1907, at the age of 84. He was buried alongside his wife and a son Frank at St. Jerome's Catholic Church cemetery in Columbus, Wisconsin. He was well remembered especially by the older inhabitants of Columbus, he being gifted with more than the average wit of his race. Courtesy of Mr. and Mrs. Vernon Barry.

MOTHER BARRY (Bridgett Brophy) born in Ireland. She was well acquainted with the Barry family. Her mother worked for Edmund's mother and sisters as a serving girl and lace maker. She married Edmund Barry and migrated to the United States in 1847, and subsequently settled in Honeoye Falls, Monroe County, New York. She bore Edmund nine children. Bridgette died on October 31, 1891, at the age of 56, and was buried in St. Jerome's Catholic Church cemetery in Columbus, Wisconsin. Courtesy of Mr. and Mrs. Vernon Barry.

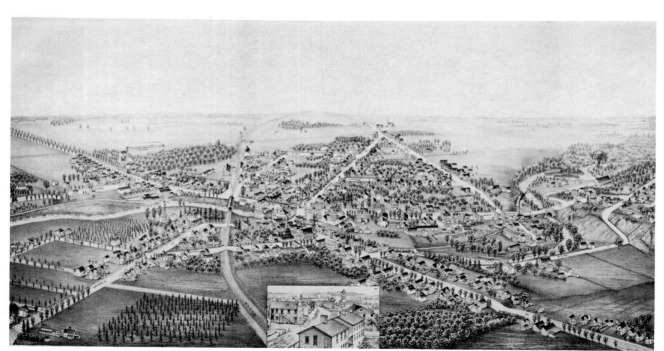

HONEOYE FALLS, NEW YORK. In 1791, Zebulon Norton bought 1,820 acres in and around the site where Honeoye Falls was later to be built. He built a cabin and in 1792 erected a grist mill by the falls. In time a village gradually appeared around the mill and it was later called Norton's Mill. Norton's Mill was the predecessor of West Mendon. On March 13, 1838, the village of West Mendon became the incorporated village of Honeoye Falls by act of the New York State legislature. Village life from earliest times was centered around Honeoye Creek. Courtesy of the Honeoye Falls-Mendon Historical Society.

CHAPTER ONE
EARLY YEARS

The Barry ancestors migrated from France with the name of DuBarry and settled in Ireland.

Due to internal problems in Ireland including no doubt the potato famine, many Irishmen migrated to other countries.

In 1847, a young Irishman by the name of Edmund Barry migrated with his young wife to the United States settling in New York in the small village of Honeoye Falls.

The Barry family was devoutly Catholic. St. Rose's Catholic Church was opened in nearby Lima in 1849. Prior to this, Catholics had to travel all the way to Rochester for church, and the services of a priest. Lima was a mission church of St. Agnes until 1853, when a resident pastor was appointed by the name of Father Quigley. He was able to pay closer attention to the mission station in Honeoye Falls. The Barrys visited Father Quigley in 1851, and had their first son John baptized.

On June 27, 1855, the census of Honeoye Falls collected the following information on the Edmund Barry family:

Edmund, 26, born Ireland, shoemaker, lived in Mendon 6 years

Bridgett, 20, born Ireland, here 6 years

John, 4, born here

James, 3, born here

David, 1 year 2 months, born here

Catherine, 30, sister of Edmund, born Ireland, here 5 years

It is the third son that is of interest. David Frances Barry was born March 6, 1854. The name Frances was in honor of his mother's father. Father Brophy had black hair, hazel eyes, rosy cheeks, and an Irish temper; traits that David inherited. It is uncertain exactly when the census was taken. If it was taken on June 27, 1855, David Barry would have been 1 year, 3 months. Even at an early age, controversy followed the lad.

Early settlers moved by the pioneer spirit headed west to seek a better life. Many stopped in Wisconsin as they traveled from New York and other eastern states.

The Barrys undertook the journey west in 1861 and settled in Ostego, Wisconsin. The shoemaker business wasn't very good. Times were hard, due in part to the Civil War being fought in the east. In 1862, Edmund moved the family to Columbus, Wisconsin.

Edmund worked at many different odd jobs to support his rapidly growing family. The children as they grew older helped out as much as they could.

Some of the boys worked for other people in order to add to the meager income.

David helped by carrying water to an itinerant photographer who had an upstairs gallery in Columbus.

The photographer O. S. Goff, traveled from place to place taking photographs in many of the small towns while working out of Portage, Wisconsin. It was through this simple job that young Barry was introduced to the basic fundamentals of the business.

On June 8, 1870, the census was taken at Columbus, Wisconsin. The Barry family included:

Edmund, 46, shoemaker, born Ireland
Bridgette, 40, housekeeper
James, 18, born New York
David, 16, born New York
Julia, 10, born New York
Ellen, 8, born New York
Edmund, 6, born Wisconsin
Margaret, 5, born Wisconsin
Michael, 2, born Wisconsin

MAIN STREET, HONEOYE FALLS 1859. In the old days, Honeoye Falls achieved a reputation as a rip-roaring town that boasted seven saloons and on Saturday nights it wasn't uncommon to see street fights and barroom brawls. Drunken revelers were confined to the village jail known as the "lockup", ironically placed opposite the Methodist Church. It was the home of young Barry until 1862. Courtesy of the Honeoye Falls-Mendon Historical Society.

CHAPTER THREE
FRONTIER PHOTOGRAPHER

Frontier photographer Orlando Scott Goff was born in East Haddam, Middlesex Co., Connecticut, on September 10, 1843, where he spent his early childhood.

During the Civil War, at 17 years of age, he ran away and joined the Tenth Connecticut Infantry serving in Company D from September 1861-September 1865.

After the war, he went home, but found life boring so after six months he decided to move west. He migrated to Lyons, N.Y. and subsequently traveled west to Portage, Wisconsin.

Goff learned the art of photography in or around Lyons, N.Y. While at Portage, he traveled as a semi-itinerant photographer.

In 1871, Goff moved to Yankton, Dakota Territory, by way of Sioux City, Iowa, and presided over the first photograph gallery in Yankton. He arrived in Burleigh County in 1872 at about the time the preliminary survey of the Northern Pacific Railroad was pushing west from the Missouri River. After spending a short time at Forts Buford and Stevenson, he returned to Fort Lincoln, which was being built on the west side of the Missouri.

Goff set up a studio in Bismarck in October 1873. On Wednesday, October 15, 1873, the Bismarck Tribune printed a new advertisement:

"Photograph Gallery O. S. Goff, artist, announces that he has located in Bismarck on Main Street, next to Tippies, where he is prepared to take orders in every branch of his profession. Orders solicited. No poor work allowed to leave the gallery. Prices reasonable."

A month later, the Tribune had this to say of Goff:

"O. S. Goff the artist, who has been "doing" the upper Missouri and Yellowstone Country in his line, has finally located at Bismarck. This gentleman is a genuine workman, as can be seen by visiting his gallery and examining his stereoscopic views, photographs of noted Indians, army officer, etc. While you are there have your picture taken and send to your friends, for life is "uncertain", and friendship fleeting unless probed occasionally by a gentle reminder."

Mr. Goff not only stayed in Bismarck, but often visited forts Lincoln and McKeen. He bought an interest in the Fort Lincoln gallery owned by a man named Ford. He moved from Bismarck to the Fort on November 5, 1873.

In the fall of 1875, Goff visited the east and when he returned he brought with him a bride, the former Miss Annie Eaton of Chestertown, N.Y., whom he had met while she was a student in the Sherwood School of Music at Lyons, N.Y. from which she had recently graduated.

Goff and his bride moved to their quarters at Fort Lincoln where he continued to take his photographs of the "Custer Clan", different officers and men, as well as the inside and outside of the Custer home.

A person that was musically endowed was a rarity on the lonely outposts of civilization. The Goffs presumably became good friends with the Custers and the other officers and wives of the regiment.

On May 17, 1876, the Seventh Cavalry, under the command of General Terry left Ft. Lincoln as part of the Yellowstone Expedition to round up the hostiles and move them to their respective agencies.

The expedition resulted in the death of Custer and five companies of cavalry and a short-lived victory for the Indians.

After the Battle of the Little Big Horn, Goff continued to take photographs around Ft. Lincoln and up-river forts as well as Bismarck. In 1876 he made a birds-eye photograph of Bismarck for Jewell's First Annual Directory.

Mrs. Goff started a singing class on Thursday and Saturday evenings. She gave instructions at the Presbyterian Church of Bismarck.

On Wednesday, February 21, 1877, the Bismarck Tribune ran an article on page 4:

"Mrs. O. S. Goff is getting along nicely with her singing class and several voices have been immensely improved under her instructions. If Mr. G. does not locate at Bismarck instead of remaining at the military posts he deserves to be confined to S. B. and hardtack for six months. Mrs. Goff would be a valuable addition to Bismarck society."

Mr. Goff realizing that Mrs. Goff was entrenched in the social functions of Bismarck, discontinued the business at Ft. Lincoln and moved permanently to the growing city of Bismarck.

The newspapers and magazines were almost begging for news from the western plains after the disastrous Yellowstone Expedition and were willing to pay handsomely for photographs of Indians and military men.

Goff decided to cash in on this bonanza and take the field again. It was a period of indecision for him. He wanted badly to tour the military posts and agencies, but he couldn't do that and run the gallery in Bismarck. After

THE DAKOTA BLOCK. O. S. Goff, Peter Thompson and Dr. H. R. Porter built the Dakota Block. Each owner financed the construction of their portion of the building. Goff's addition extended only part way back on the second floor. There was a photographer's studio in the back portion of the second floor with a large skylight above. Barry leased the photograph gallery of Goff's portion in 1884. Courtesy of the North Dakota State Historical Society.

FIRE INSURANCE MAP. Showing the Dakota and Anderson Blocks on Main street. Goff owned lot #703. The skylight and photographic gallery can be seen on the back portion of the second floor. Courtesy of the North Dakota State Historical Society.

some serious deliberation, he decided to have someone run his gallery while he sought photographs. He contacted David Barry, the young Wisconsin lad who had shown an interest in photography back in Columbus, Wisconsin.

Thus D. F. Barry entered the photography profession during the wet plate days in 1878 as a protegé of frontier photographer Orlando Scott Goff.

This period of Barry's life is rather cloudy. In 1870 Goff was in and around Portage, Wisconsin. He operated as a traveling photographer visiting all of the small towns periodically. Presumably he visited nearby Columbus in his travels and employed young Barry to carry water and do other odd jobs for him while in Columbus. He probably saw in the lad the same restlessness that he had experienced.

A further search for Barry from 1870 until 1878 proved futile. Numerous city directories and historical societies were checked to no avail.

It is highly probable that Barry drifted from job to job after Goff moved west trying to find his true calling. His

chance came in 1878. Goff probably contacted Barry and urged him to come west and help him in his Bismarck gallery. The earliest mention of Barry in Dakota is 1878.

Goff showed Barry the finer points of photography and was then free to tour the forts knowing full well that his interests were being looked after. Goff also decided to make some improvements to his traveling equipment. He made up a portable gallery affixed to a wagon that could be pulled easily and gave him a wider range in which to procure photographs.

Barry became an apprentice, business partner, employee to Goff and started to make his way in the not-so-old art of photography.

On Friday, Sept. 12, 1879, Goff went to Fort Meade to spend the fall and possibly winter in driving his photographing business. Barry was left in charge of his Bismarck establishment.

David F. Barry was on his own!

Thursday, July 1, 1880, the Fargo Times had this to say:

"O. S. Goff and wife, of Bismarck, stopped over,

ORLANDO SCOTT GOFF—THE OLD MASTER. He taught Barry the finer points of photography and gave him the confidence that catapulted him on his way. Photo by Goff, a self-photograph. Courtesy of the North Dakota State Historical Society.

MRS. ORLANDO S. GOFF. Annie Eaton of Chestertown, N.Y. met Orlando Goff when she was a student in the Sherwood School of Music at Lyons, N.Y. from which she had recently graduated. The newlyweds moved to Ft. Lincoln where Goff had a studio and subsequently to Bismarck. O.S. Goff photo. Courtesy of the North Dakota State Historical Society.

while waiting for a train on Monday evening. They passed west through Fargo five years ago. The changes almost bewildered them. Mr. Goff is ready to wager one of his many town lots that the country between the Missouri and Yellowstone will be similarly settled and improved in the next 5 years. They are on a tour of the Lakes, the St. Lawrence, Lake Champlain and Saratoga. It is a grand trip. The writer once took it in his imagination."

Presumably Goff at this time was a man of property. The Bismarck Tribune on July 30, 1880, stated that Cliff Brothers, the artists, have removed their store, now occupying a portion of Mr. Goff's building on Main Street. Everything in the shape of paints and oils they have.

In 1881, Sitting Bull and the last of his followers surrendered at Ft. Buford and were on their way south on the steamer "General Sherman". They were scheduled to stop at Bismarck on August 1.

Judson Elliot Walker, who was writing a book titled "Campaigns of General Custer in the Northwest and the Final Surrender of Sitting Bull", approached Goff and asked him if he would photograph Sitting Bull. Goff consented.

At the hotel, the chief and his friends were given a good dinner. Then Sitting Bull was asked to go to the gallery of Goff, the town's leading photographer, to have his photograph taken. At first the chief was superstitious about having Goff take his photo. Finally, after a promise of $50 for one shot, he consented. Sitting stiffly upright and holding his pipe across his arms, he let Goff make one negative, then, collecting his $50, he hastily left the studio.

Goff was one of the leading citizens of Bismarck. In 1883, he and Dr. H. R. Porter, "The hero of the Little Big Horn" along with Peter Thompson, decided to build a building.

The building was dubbed the "Dakota Block" and was 75 × 85 feet, three stories high, and included a full-sized basement. The fronts were of pressed brick or terra cotta. Each owner owned a 25 foot lot and apparently financed the construction of their portion of the building. On Goff's addition the third story extended

FT. ASSINIBOINE, MONTANA. Goff opened a studio in Havre, Montana, with a branch at Ft. Assiniboine. He visited the fort once a month to take photographs of the soldiers stationed there. Goff kept visiting the fort until the soldiers were withdrawn for service in Cuba during the Spanish American War. Photo by Barry. Courtesy of the Denver Public Library, Western History Dept.

only part way back. There was a photographer's studio in the back portion of the second floor with a large skylight above.

There was no art that had been more improved than that of the photographer. O. S. Goff kept up with the times. He erected his portion of the building especially for his business and provided for the arrangement of light.

The new building was on the corner of Main and Second Streets opposite Camp Hancock, the Quartermaster Depot on Main Street.

Goff also advertised in Dan Eisenberg's show window, next door to the post office, as well as in the newspapers.

Goff at this time still wasn't content to settle in his new building. In the early spring of 1884, he rented his new photographer's gallery to David Barry.

Mr. Goff left Bismarck and began a career as a semi-itinerant photographer at a number of military posts in Montana starting at Ft. Custer in 1884. In the later part of June, he was quoted as saying:

"No one can appreciate the thrift and prosperity of Bismarck and the Missouri Valley until a trip is taken over the country. Crops in Dakota and around Bismarck are much farther advanced and in a far better condition than anywhere along the line."

On the 27th of June, Goff left on the steamer "Helena" for Fort Assiniboine. He remained there until the demand for pictures ended.

He returned to Bismarck in October to spend the winter months after sojourning at the various forts.

On December 26, 1884, it was announced that O. S. Goff was elected High Priest of the Missouri Chapter No. 6, Royal Arch Masons. Other elected officials included: Excellent King Carl T. Peterson; Excellent Scribe Charles R. Williams; Treasurer James H. Marshall; and Secretary E. M. Fuller.

Mrs. Goff was still actively involved in the social functions of the city. At a special meeting of the Bismarck Library Association the following were elected to hold the office until the election of officers in January:

President Mrs. O. S. Goff; Vice President Mrs.

SITTING BULL. A painting of the first photograph of Sitting Bull taken by O. S. Goff August 1, 1881, while the Indians stopped in Bismarck on their way south. In the later 1890's, a fire swept the Goff studio in Havre, Montana. Among the priceless relics burned or stolen was this picture, which had been exhibited in the Dakota Building at the World's Columbian Exposition in Chicago in 1893, and Sitting Bull's pipe which he was holding when the photograph was taken. Courtesy of the North Dakota State Historical Society.

W. M. Pye; Sec. Vice Pres. C. H. Clague; Treasurer Mrs. C. S. Weaver; and Secretary Mrs. F. J. Call.

Goff spent a year and one-half in a Chicago hospital when an old Civil War wound began troubling him.

He opened a studio in Havre, Montana, with a branch at Ft. Assiniboine, where he visited once a month to take photographs of the soldiers stationed there. In 1896 he was in and around Dickinson, North Dakota. He kept visiting Ft. Assiniboine until the soldiers were withdrawn for service in Cuba during the Spanish American War.

He continued his work at Havre until a fire swept his studio. Among the priceless relics burned or stolen during the confusion caused by the fire was a huge enlargement of the first picture of Sitting Bull, which had been exhibited in the Dakota Building at the World's Columbian Exposition, in Chicago in 1893, and Sitting Bull's pipe which he was holding when the picture was taken.

In 1900, Goff retired from the photography business. He continued to live in Montana and was elected to the State Legislature in 1905. His last years were spent in Idaho where he died in 1917.

O. S. GOFF,

PHOTOGRAPHER

— OF —

SITTING BULL, CHIEF JOSEPH,

AND ALL THE HOSTILE SIOUX CHIEFS.

Also, the Finest Collection of Indian Photos in America.

Correspondence Solicited.   **BISMARCK, D. T.**

CHAPTER FOUR
BISMARCK

As civilization pushed unceasingly west in 1870, the Northern Pacific Railroad was in the vanguard making a determined effort to attract settlers to railroad lands. It established an agency in London, England, and distributed literature on Dakota Territory all over Europe and the eastern United States. Railroad lands were offered on attractive installment terms: 10 percent down and seven years to pay the balance.

In anticipation, the railroad built large reception houses as temporary homes for land seekers at Duluth, Glyndon and Brainerd. Free transportation was also offered to purchasers of Northern Pacific lands.

Squatters anticipating the coming of the Northern Pacific spent the winter of 1871-1872 in the vicinity of what was later to become Bismarck.

As the railroad pushed closer toward the Missouri River, a small cluster of shacks accumulated near the river. This group of shacks was given the name Edwinton, in honor of a relative of one of the directors of the Lake Superior and Puget Sound Company. As the railroad arrived, the name was changed to Bismarck in honor of the German Chancellor. It was hoped that the new name would attract German capital and settlers.

During 1872, a considerable amount of building went on in Bismarck.

That year the Army located at Camp Greely (later Camp Hancock) to protect the railroad construction crews from hostile Indians.

About this time most of the country around Bismarck was unoccupied except for attaches of the military posts, Indian agencies and an occasional woodchopper on the Missouri River.

Fort Rice, 30 miles below Bismarck, was the principle military post. Fort McKeen, an infantry post was built in 1872 across the Missouri River opposite Bismarck to protect the builders of the Northern Pacific. The name was changed in 1873 to Fort Abraham Lincoln when the cavalry post was built on the flat below.

In July of 1873 the county of Burleigh was organized. John P. Dunn, Wm. H. H. Mercer and James A. Emmons were elected as county commissioners. Other elected officials were Dan Williams — Register of Deeds; I. S. Carville — Judge of Probate; John E. Wasson — County Attorney; and Major Woods — Sheriff.

On June 5, 1873 the first locomotive arrived on the newly laid Northern Pacific tracks from Fargo. One of the newcomers to Bismarck was Colonel C. H. Lounsberry and his printing press. The first edition of the Bismarck Weekly Tribune was put out on July 11, 1873.

In the summer of 1873, a great financial panic swept the east and great Philadelphia Banking Firm of Jay Cooke and Co. Construction of the Northern Pacific was halted at Bismarck and didn't resume until 1878 when the Northern Pacific showed signs of pushing up the Yellowstone Valley.

Most of these railroad towns had a floating population that was rough and violent. An Army officer wrote to his wife about Bismarck "I have not fallen in love with Bismarck. It is a bad specimen of a frontier town. Nobody expects to stay here permanently, but hoping to make some money to get away with."

In the forefront of civilization there are more often than not two types of people. The first is the upright individual who is trying to make his way in the world. The other is the person that lives off of him. Bismarck was a new town and these two groups did exist.

Mrs. George A. Custer in 1873 wrote of Bismarck, "When we finally reached the termination of the road at Bismarck, another train was just about to start back to St. Paul. The street was full of people widely expostulating and talking loudly and fiercely. It appeared that this was the last train of the season, as the cars were not to run during the winter. The passengers were mostly Bismarck citizens, whose lawless life as gamblers and murderers had so enraged the sentiments of the few law-abiding residents that they had forced them to depart. We could see these outlaws crowding at the door, hanging out of the windows, swearing and menacing; and finally firing

on the retreating crowd as the cars passed out of town."

Pvt. A. Frank Mulford described Bismarck as he disembarked the train for Ft. Lincoln in 1876. "Bismarck was a thriving town of about 5,000 inhabitants. It was notorious for its many dance halls, gambling dens and crime holes of all kinds. There was a large floating population of the worst characters from the east and reckless frontier toughs. Brawls and murders were frequent, mostly due to the consumption of a vicious whiskey manufactured not far from town."

As Bismarck grew into an upstanding community many families looked down upon the crime holes and "blind pigs".

Mrs. M. H. Jewell had this to say about Fourth Street. "Fourth Street was also known as "Murderers gulch" and with the coming of the Seventh Cavalry to Ft. Lincoln, the character of Bismarck changed materially for the worst."

Many of these raw little towns, especially at the end of the railroad, were rough places where drifters, prostitutes, sporting houses and gambling establishments ran

BISMARCK JUNE 1873. Squatters anticipating the coming of the Northern Pacific Railroad spent the winter of 1871-1872 in the vicinity of what was later to become Bismarck. As the railroad pushed closer toward the Missouri River, a small cluster of shacks and tents accumulated near the river. Courtesy of the North Dakota State Historical Society.

CHAPTER FIVE
LAST STAND OF THE
RED MAN 1877-1881

After their triumphant victory of 1876, the hostile Indian tribes scattered to the four directions to escape pursuit by government troops. Some of the tribes fled north to the safety of the British possessions. Many kept crossing the border and committing depredations as far south as the Yellowstone and, when pursued by troops, would escape again into the Northwest Territory.

These were hard times for the hostiles. They were constantly hunted by soldiers and couldn't stop long enough to hunt or make new lodges. Many returned to the reservations, persuaded by their relatives that no harm would come to them.

The winter successes of Crook, McKenzie, and Miles in 1876 foreshadowed the end of the Sioux War. In April of 1877, one-thousand Sioux led by Touch-the-Clouds surrendered at Spotted Tail Agency and Dull Knife brought his Cheyennes into Camp Robinson.

On April 22, 1877, three-hundred Indians led by Two Moons and Hump surrendered to Col. Miles.

Emissaries to the hostile camps brought back word that Crazy Horse was also on his way in.

Captain John G. Bourke had this to say of Crazy Horse. "He would probably never have surrendered, had it not been for the defections around him, the defeat of the Cheyennes by McKenzie, and the destruction of so much of his camp equipage at Wolf Mt. He possibly might also have continued the fighting if his warriors weren't freezing, starving, and out of ammunition."

Crazy Horse, Little Hawk and the others of his band moved southward and surrendered at Red Cloud and Spotted Tail agencies in May of 1877.

When Crazy Horse and his band came in and surrendered, he formed all of his warriors in line, in advance of his women and children; then in front of this line, ten or more of his headmen; and in front of these he rode.

He had 889 men, women and children with him. They reluctantly gave up 2,000 ponies and 217 men turned in 117 rifles and pistols.

Crazy Horse acted in a manner which aroused suspicion on the part of military authorities at Camp Robinson. The soldiers described his attitude as sullen and restless despite his expressed desire for peace. Some chiefs of the agency bands also found his increasing popularity among their followers as a threat to their positions.

Even though Crazy Horse had surrendered he soon again became the favorite of many of the reservation Indians. They knew that whatever he had done was for the benefit of his people.

The others fearing they would lose their importance became jealous of him. They held many secret meetings and plotted against him, claiming that he was conspiring to assassinate General Crook.

Quietly, his blanket folded over his arm as though he was going to his lodge between two friends, Crazy Horse let himself be taken past a soldier walking up and down with a bayonet gun on his shoulder and in through a door...only then did he see the barred windows, the men with chains on their legs, and realize it was the iron house. Like a grizzly, he jumped back, drawing the hidden gift knife to strike out around him, but Little Big Man grabbed his arms from behind so he wouldn't get hurt. In the melee he was fatally wounded by a bayonet thrust and died shortly before midnight on Sept. 5, 1877, in the adjutant's office. His parents took the body of their son and secretly buried it.

There now remained hostile only those under Sitting Bull and his lieutenants, Black Moon, Gall, Rain-in-the-Face, Spotted Tail, and White Eagle, as they were under the protection of the British border.

Life was quiet during the winter months. Both Goff and Barry worked the gallery in Bismarck and developed many plates they had acquired during the previous summer. In the spring which sometimes comes early in Dakota, they would alternately work the forts and agencies.

On April 8, 1881, Goff took charge of the Bismarck gallery and Barry visited Ft. Buford and other upriver points.

Goff decided to expand his business, so he traveled downriver to Standing Rock Agency, later named Ft. Yates in honor of one of Custer's officers. While at the agency, he made arrangements for rooms so they could take photographs. Goff, at this time with Barry's help, had the finest collection of Indian portraits seen anywhere. He was offered a small fortune for the negatives, but declined to sell.

It was during this time Barry had a brain storm. After working with Goff for a few years, he had picked up much. Goff had a gallery that was affixed to a wagon and could be driven around. Barry decided to make a portable gallery. He had it built in St. Paul. It was prefabricated so it could be put up and taken down easily. He then could transport it on a steamboat and unload it at the location where he wished to set up. It was a faster

MAJOR JAMES MCLAUGHLIN, Indian Agent at Standing Rock Agency. He settled the Sioux at Standing Rock Agency and broke them to the ways of the white man. He used Indians against Indians to his advantage. From the moment he and Sitting Bull met, they were at odds with each other. Photo by Barry. Courtesy of the Douglas County Historical Museum.

TATANKA YOTANKA, Sitting Bull. It was through his influence as a medicine man that many joined the hostiles and subsequently moved to the Little Big Horn. Photo by Barry. Courtesy of the Douglas County Historical Museum.

THE FIRST PHOTOGRAPH OF CHIEF GALL 1881. While at Fort Buford, Barry took this photograph of Gall. While in the process of developing it, Gall returned to the studio and wanted to destroy it. While searching for it, Gall pulled a knife on him and Barry grabbed a revolver. Both eyed each other. Gall left the studio. Later Barry took many other photographs of Gall and they became friends, but neither referred to the Fort Buford affair. Photo by Barry. Courtesy of the Douglas County Historical Museum.

41

WAR EAGLE. Photo by Barry. Courtesy of the Smithsonian Institution, National Anthropological Archives, Bureau of American Ethnology Collection.

way of transporting his equipment. He worked at this idea and was successful with it.

Goff was often called upon to take pictures of buildings. He photographed the New Church of the Bread of Life, both exterior and interior. The interior showed the fine floral decorations artistically arranged and displayed for Easter Sunday.

On May 6, Barry bid his many friends adieu, and left on the Far West for Ft. Buford. He took his portable gallery with him.

In September 1880, a scout named "Fish" Allison was dispatched by the government from Ft. Buford to communicate with Sitting Bull and other chiefs with the intention of inducing them to surrender. He made several visits to the hostiles and consequently many came reluctantly to Poplar River Agency, Montana, late in 1880.

Big Road and 200 Sioux, among them Rain-in-the-Face, surrendered to the commanding officer at Ft. Keogh, Montana, September 8, 1880.

Some of the Indians, after they had collected in force, became turbulent and arrogant and assumed a threatening attitude toward the small garrison at Poplar River.

On Dec. 15, 1880, fearing another Indian uprising, Major Guido Ilges, with five mounted companies marched nearly 200 miles through deep snow, with the temperature resting at 10-35 degrees below zero to reinforce the Poplar River garrison.

Maj. Ilges was ordered on Jan. 2, 1881, to move against some camps of Sioux located on the opposite side of the Missouri. The Indians fled from the village, and took refuge in some timber, from which they were driven by a few shells from two artillery pieces and surrendered.

This group of Indians consisted of chiefs Gall, Low Dog, and Crow King with their bands reluctantly bound from Canada. They gave up nearly 200 ponies, together with 69 rifles and pistols as well as a considerable amount of camp equipment. After this surrender, little bands of Indians began filtering into Ft. Buford or Camp Poplar River to give themselves up.

The Indians were sent to Fort Buford as prisoners of war, and on the long march suffered much, for they were poorly clad and the weather was severe.

CHIEF OLD WOLF. Courtesy of the Douglas County Historical Museum.

CHIEF LITTLE JOHN. Photo by Barry. In the author's collection.

43

When Barry heard that Gall had surrendered and was heading for Ft. Buford, he took his portable gallery and started upriver. He had long wanted Gall's photograph. Barry said, "Upon my arrival I reported to Maj. Brotherton and made my business known to him. He gave me permission to take photographs of the Indians, and informed me that I was subject to orders the same as anyone else at the post. He cautioned me against giving the Indians any information regarding the movements or plans of the troops or of the movements of Indians that I might hear of from the officers and above all warned me to avoid having any trouble with any of the Indians. I had my portable gallery with me and proceeded to set up. I was more than anxious to photograph Chief Gall. I went to the hostile camp and through the interpreter "Fish" Allison made arrangements to take photographs of the chiefs at $6.00 per sitting."

The interpreter, failing to make money for himself, told the chiefs that Barry would get rich with their photographs, whereupon Gall raised his price to $21.00 with a little help. Barry reluctantly agreed to pay the sum.

Gall came to the gallery as he was dressed at camp with no preparation of any kind. He was accompanied by Captain Clifford and scout Flurey. He refused to listen to suggestions as to how to pose. Barry took two photographs—one sitting and one standing. Gall stood before the camera as best suited him. He pulled his robe over his head with only his eyes showing. Realizing that such a photograph would be worthless, Barry gently pulled the robe down over his shoulders and rolled back his shirt, baring his magnificent chest. Gall with a haughty, scornful attitude eyed Barry with disdain and, at that moment, Barry snapped the shutter.

Later Gall returned to the gallery alone and asked to see the photograph. Barry only had the glass plate and didn't make a print off it. Barry decided not to show him and Gall decided to find it himself, no doubt to destroy it because it was "bad medicine".

Realizing that all his work and money was in peril, Barry pushed the chief away from the darkroom. Gall pulled his knife and was about to end Barry's career when Barry picked up a revolver. Seeing the determina-

COTTON MAN, a warrior who fought Custer's troops and took one of their carbines. Photo by Barry. Courtesy of the Denver Public Library, Western History Dept.

Chief Hairy-Chin

Meeting of the Constitutional Convention at Bismarck, North Dakota, on July 4th, 1889

All the noted Sioux chiefs at Standing Rock were invited to attend and be the guests of the city and take part in the parade. The following chiefs were in the parade: Chief Gall, Rain-in-the-Face, John Grass, Goose, Mad Bear, Running Antelope, Black Bull, Circling Bear, Crow Eagle, Flying Bye, Sitting Bull, Two Bear, Long Dog, Fire Cloud, Long Feather, Low Dog, Crow King, High Bear, Gray Eagle, Crow, Fool Thunder, Red Horse and Red Fish.

Major McLoughlin was in command of the chiefs and dressed Hairy Chin to appear as Uncle Sam and to lead the parade. Two days after they had returned to Standing Rock, Hairy Chin died. He was a brother to Chief Long Dog. The Indians claimed he dressed and appeared as Uncle Sam, which was bad medicine, and was the cause of Hairy Chin taking that old trail to the Happy Hunting Grounds.

Never again will they get a Sioux to parade as Uncle Sam. While at Bismarck they were looked after by D. F. Barry. He feared perhaps he had over-fed them—the end of Hairy Chin.

D. F. BARRY

Photographer of Noted Indians

1312 Tower Ave.

SUPERIOR,   WISCONSIN

D. F. BARRY

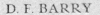

tion on the face of Barry, Gall left the gallery.

In less than an hour, Barry was summoned into the presence of the commanding officer where Gall had reported that Barry wanted to shoot him. Barry had been warned on his admittance to the fort to avoid any trouble with the Indians. It was only owing to his diplomacy in denying the incident that he was not deprived of his privilege of remaining at the fort.

Later Barry and Gall became good friends at Standing Rock Agency and Barry photographed him many times. However, neither ever referred to the Fort Buford affair.

Elizabeth B. Custer wrote a note to Barry when she saw Gall's photograph knowing full well that he was one of the Indians that killed her husband and all of the men in his command.

"Mr. Barry:

Painful as it is for me to look upon a pictured face of an Indian, I have never dreamed in all my life, there could be so fine a speciman of a warrior, in all the tribes as Chief Gall."

Mrs. Elizabeth B. Custer

Other tributes are as follows:

"The photograph of Chief Gall, with his head and body unadorned by savage finery of any kind, with his buffalo robes thrown back, baring his magnificent torso, is one of the most striking of all Indian pictures, and it is a speaking likeness too, looking just as if he had stepped forth to address his people."

Gen. Chas. King

"The greatest and strongest Indian face that I have ever seen."

—Trentanova
The Sculptor, of Florence Italy

Barry said of his photograph of Gall:

"The monarch Chief, with the Daniel Webster face of all the North American Indians."

Barry also took many photographs at Ft. Buford during the time he was there. He took a photograph of Chief Crow King wearing Maj. Brotherton's coat. At this time there remained only one hostile group left. This group was led by Sitting Bull.

On July 19, Sitting Bull with the last of his followers,

STEAMER F. Y. BATCHELOR with troops from Ft. Yates. After the Indian surrender, the Indians were brought down river to Standing Rock Agency on river boats. Courtesy of the North Dakota State Historical Society.

comprising 45 men, 67 women and 73 children surrendered to the commanding officer at Fort Buford, D.T.

"On July 14, 1881, a dispatch was received from Fort Buford, D.T.: Gen. A. H. Terry, Commanding Dept. Dakota, Ft. Snelling: Just received a dispatch from Legare, dated 12th inst.; says he is enroute with Sitting Bull, Four Horns and Red Thunder; in all 6 chiefs, 40 families, about 200 in all. He says they came from Lake Qu'Appele, starving. Will send in this to meet them with rations. Messenger says they are about sixty miles out." (signed) D. H. Brotherton, Maj. 7th Infantry Commanding Officer.

Through the efforts of a scout, Louis Legare, Sitting Bull was induced to come into the lines and surrender to the military.

They arrived at Fort Buford. At the head of the mournful cortege rode Sitting Bull, Four Horns, Red Thunder and other sub-chiefs, on their war ponies, following them came six Army wagons loaded with the women and children and behind them came some twenty-five of Louis Legare's Red River carts, containing their baggage.

They presented a forlorn and pitiful appearance. Sitting Bull was very dirty and hungry looking. His dress and appearance bore marks of hardships and destitution.

Fort Buford, D. T. July 19

"General A. H. Terry, Commanding Dept. of Dakota, Ft. Snelling:
Sitting Bull and his followers surrendered to me at noon today."
 (signed) D. H. Brotherton, Maj. 7th Infantry Com.

The steamboat, General Sherman, brought Sitting Bull and all of the surrendered hostiles from Fort Buford down river to Standing Rock Agency. On the way, the steamer stopped at Bismarck. A large party of white people boarded the boat to see Sitting Bull. Among them were Col. Clement Lounsberry, publisher of the Tribune; H. F. Douglas, post trader at Standing Rock; several Army officers from Fort Abraham Lincoln; and a number of women and children. A short time later, the whole party of Sioux was taken ashore for an issue of rations.

Sitting Bull and other leaders were loaded in wagons

CROW KING. As one of Sitting Bull's followers, he fought Custer at the Little Big Horn. Photo by Barry. Courtesy of the Denver Public Library. Western History Dept.

CHIEF WILD HORSE reputed to be the cousin of Crazy Horse. Photo by Barry. Courtesy of the Douglas County Historical Museum.

to be taken to the hotel to be dined and shown around the city.

At this time, Barry was at Ft. Buford when the Indians were removed to Standing Rock Agency. Barry wired the only report to M. H. Jewell of the Bismarck Tribune, who then wired it to the press.

Barry probably cursed his luck when he was at Fort Buford and failed to get the first photograph of Sitting Bull. In years to come, Barry took many photographs of him.

INDIAN DEAD. Photo by Barry. In the author's collection.

INDIAN VILLAGE. After their triumphant victory of 1876, the hostile Indian tribes scattered to escape pursuit by government troops. These were hard times for the Indians. They were constantly hunted by soldiers and couldn't stop long enough to hunt or make new lodges. Photo believed to be by Barry. Courtesy of the Douglas County Historical Museum.

CROOKED FACE AND FAMILY. Photo by Barry. Courtesy of the Smithsonian Institution, National Anthropological Archives, Bureau of American Ethnology Collection.

RAIN-IN-THE-FACE, Big Road and 200 Sioux surrendered to the commanding officer at Ft. Keogh, Montana, Sept. 8, 1880, reluctantly bound from Canada. Photo by Barry. Courtesy of the Smithsonian Institution, National Anthropological Archives, Bureau of American Ethnology Collection.

CHAPTER SIX
GUARDIANS OF THE MISSOURI

FORT RICE

Without the encouragement of officers and men at the various military posts, Goff and Barry couldn't have compiled their large assortment of valuable photographs.

These "Guardian Angels" on the fringe of civilization raised the hopes of many a traveler along the Missouri River or into the unknown Dakota Territory.

Military posts, which stood in many cases alone, away from civilization, guarded the territory and interests of enterprising individuals as they pushed the frontier back.

The Military Division of the Missouri was established Jan. 30, 1865, by General Orders No. 11, War Department, Series of 1865. It then included the Departments of the Missouri and the Northwest. On March 21, 1865, the Dept. of Arkansas and Indian Territory were added to it.

On June 27, 1865, the Division of the Missouri was merged into the Division of the Mississippi, embracing the Depts. of the Ohio, Missouri and of the Arkansas; headquartered at St. Louis on August 6, 1866, the name of the Division was changed to "Military Division of the Missouri", comprising the Depts. of the Arkansas, Missouri, Platte, and a new department to be created, Dakota.

The Dept. of Dakota comprised the state of Minnesota and the territories of Dakota and Montana.

To garrison the military posts and to furnish troops for field operations, the present force in the division comprised eight regiments of cavalry, twenty regiments of infantry and one battery of artillery, totaling 15,940 officers and men.

Several factors were usually considered in the selection of sites for forts. The factors included: availability of drinking water, grass for forage, timber for building, fuel and a sufficient tract of level land for a parade ground, barracks, officer quarters, storehouses, stables and other buildings. In the Missouri River posts, it was also necessary to choose a site near a good steamboat landing.

Most of the earlier posts were made of local building materials, and the labor "generously" furnished by soldiers.

Some of the earlier posts were built of logs such as Fort Rice, Totten, Grand River, Lower Brule, and Cheyenne River Agencies. Others such as forts Robinson, Stevenson, Niobrara, Buford and Shaw were built partly or entirely out of adobe.

In 1873, when the Seventh Cavalry was moving to its new post at Fort Abraham Lincoln, it stopped at Fort Rice. Mrs. George A. Custer made this observation: "A rickety old ferry boat took us across the river when we made a halt near Ft. Rice. Strange to say the river was no narrower than it was so many hundreds of miles below where we started. The river was muddy, and full of sand bars. We bravely began to drink the

50

water, when the glass had been filled long enough for the sediment to partially settle. We learned after a time to settle the water with alum and finally became accustomed to the taste."

The quarters were very ordinary frame buildings, with no modern improvements. They were painted a funeral tint, but one warranted to last.

Fort Rice was established in 1864 on the right or west bank of the Missouri River. It was rebuilt in 1868. A stockade of gray cottonwood logs offered protection during an attack. Four companies of Seventh Cavalry were stationed there commanded by Col. Joseph G. Tilford.

In 1868, commissioners stopped at Fort Rice and attempted to pursuade the Sioux to take up farming as part of the 1868 Laramie Treaty. Gall was sent as an emissary from Sitting Bull to attend the council. He was the first to sign the treaty.

During the late summer of 1871, Major J. N. C. Whistler and a detachment of soldiers spent a little over a month escorting a reconnaissance party from Ft. Rice to the mouth of Glendive Creek and back. They were working out the route between the Missouri Crossing at Bismarck and the Bozeman Pass. At the same time another party worked on the western end of this unsurveyed portion.

An expedition was organized under Col. D. S. Stanley to establish a supply depot near Glendive Creek where it empties into the Yellowstone, where it was expected the surveying parties of the Northern Pacific would run their line across the river.

The expedition consisted of more than 1,500 officers and men which consisted of 20 companies of infantry, and 10 companies of cavalry under Lt. Col. George A. Custer. There were 275 wagons and ambulances carrying sufficient rations and forage to last 60 days. The chief of the Northern Pacific's engineers was Custer's old West Point classmate and friend, the Confederate General Thomas L. Rosser.

The task of the surveyors in 1873 was to close up the gap between the last stake driven by Haydon's survey party and the point established by Rosser at the mouth of the Powder River.

FT. RICE-DAKOTA TERRITORY 1868; established in 1864 on the west bank of the Missouri River. It was rebuilt in 1868. The quarters were very ordinary frame buildings painted a funereal tint. It was surrounded by gray cottonwood logs which offered protection from attack. In 1868, commissioners stopped at Ft. Rice and attempted to pursuade the Sioux to take up farming as part of the Laramie Treaty. Expeditions were sent from Ft. Rice in 1871 and 1873. After 1873, Ft. Rice lived in the shadow of Ft. Lincoln, built upriver. Courtesy of the North Dakota State Historical Society.

FT. ABRAHAM LINCOLN 1873. So bold had been Indian attacks upon whites in the Dept. of Dakota that an additional regiment of cavalry, the Seventh, was transferred to that Dept. from the Military Division of the South. Accordingly, 6 additional cavalry quarters were built between the hill and the river below Ft. McKeen. Courtesy of the North Dakota State Historical Society.

Fort Rice was 28 miles south of Bismarck. Sioux City was 503 miles distant by land, and 750 miles by Missouri River. The military reservation was an area 25 miles long and 7 miles wide.

The post had quarters for four companies; eleven sets of officers quarters; a hospital; post office; guard house; library; three quartermaster storehouses; three commissary storehouses; and one ordnance. It also had two cavalry stables and four quartermaster's stables.

The buildings were built of cottonwood and pine. Generally they required repairs. The magazine was built of stone. Quartermaster stores, clothing, etc. were furnished by contract from Jeffersonville, Indiana. Subsistence stores were furnished from depots in Chicago and St. Louis. These stores were brought upriver by steamboats. The land was sterile and sparsely timbered and watered, and the soil was light and gravelly. The bottom lands were rich and moist. The climate was generally dry. Summers were short and hot, with temperatures from 90-110 degrees and winters long and cold with the temperature often around 40 degrees below zero.

For armaments Fort Rice had one (1) one-inch gatling, and one (1) one-half inch gatling gun.

In 1877 Company M Seventh Cavalry went into winter quarters at Fort Rice. With nothing to do except army routine day after day, life soon became boring.

Trumpeter A. F. Mulford described a typical day in the army at Fort Rice: "At the first streak of daylight there was first call for reveille, ten minutes later assembly would be sounded. Everyone would fall in for company parade, while the first Sgts. would take roll call.

"Mess call was at 7:30.

"At 8 o'clock, fatigue call would be sounded and the men that had been detailed the evening before would start out for the work to be done that day. The guards went to the guard house, the saddler to his little log hut, the sawmill men would go to the government mill and saw wood, the quartermaster's men would report at the storehouses, the stable police to the stables, kitchen police to the kitchens and mess room. There was always plenty to do, but none of it hard enough to hurt a man. No soldier ever overworks!

ENLISTED MEN'S BARRACKS AT FT. LINCOLN. Courtesy of the Custer Battlefield Museum.

FORT ABRAHAM LINCOLN after December 2, 1890. Photo by Z. Gilbert. Courtesy of the North Dakota State Historical Society.

WINTER AT FORT LINCOLN 1885, showing officer's row and a storehouse. Photo by Barry. Courtesy of the North Dakota State Historical Society.

OFFICER'S ROW, FT. LINCOLN, D. T. Custer's house, the second from the right, served as a gathering place for the officers and their families. Courtesy of the Custer Battlefield Museum.

GUARD MOUNT AT FORT A. LINCOLN. Photo by Haynes, June 1877. Courtesy of the North Dakota State Historical Society.

FORT ABRAHAM LINCOLN 1975. Officer's Row remains are seen by the horizontal line of trees in the center of the photo. Photo by Bob Heski.

"9 o'clock was first call for guard mounting, then assembly of guard details and trumpeters.

"The new guard would then march in review or to the guard house and take charge of the prisoners and all property that had to be guarded.

"After guard mount, water and stable calls would summon every man not on other duty to the stables. Each man wore a white frock and overalls. The horses were led to the river and watered, then returned to the stables and groomed for a whole hour under the immediate direction of the first sergeant.

"At 12 o'clock recall was sounded, and all work would be dropped and preparations made ready for dinner.

"First sergeants call would follow and the first sergeants would go to the adjutant's office and get their morning reports.

"Mess call was at 12:30.

"One o'clock would again be the time for fatigue call. Work would be continued as each would proceed to kill time, as they had been doing all the forenoon.

"If the weather was fine, drill call would be sounded at 2:30, then the men would put on their belts and sabers and their longest faces and fall in. Sometimes it would be dismounted drill and at other times mounted, and for a change we would have target practice.

"The 4 o'clock recall would announce that the time had come to cease drill and work, then the privates would don their white suits and be ready for water and stable call, which was at 4:30, when the "government ghosts" would again march to the stables to water and groom their mounts.

"At sunset, first call, then assembly would be sounded. The men would assemble on the company parades and answer to their names as they were called by the first sergeants, after which retreat would be sounded by all the trumpeters, and the evening gun would be fired at the last note.

"The men didn't have anything to do until 8:30 when first call for tatto and then assembly would call them to the parades, then the roll was called.

"Taps would be played at exactly 9 o'clock when all

FT. McKEEN-DAKOTA TERRITORY. In April of 1872, a camp was established on the west side of Sibley Island for the protection of the surveyors of the North Pacific Railroad. At first named Camp Green, the name was later changed to Ft. McKeen in honor of Col. H. Boyd McKeen, who was killed in the battle of Cold Harbor during the Civil War. Courtesy of the North Dakota State Historical Society.

GATLING GUNS AT FT. McKEEN pulled by condemned cavalry horses. Guns of this type rarely were fired at the mobile Indian tribes in the Dept. of Dakota. Courtesy of the Custer Battlefield Museum.

the lights in the men's quarters must be extinguished. All would then be still except the click of billiard balls in the Officer's club room at the sutler's.''

FORT ABRAHAM LINCOLN

In April of 1872, Captain Green was ordered up from Ft. Rice to establish a camp on the west side of Sibley Island for the protection of the surveyors of the Northern Pacific Railroad. It was known as Camp Green. Soon after, a commission was appointed consisting of Col. Daniel Huston, Quartermaster Scully and Dr. Slaughter to locate a military post. By this commission, the "old fort on the hill", was created. This fort was named Ft. McKeen, in honor of Col. H. Boyd McKeen, who was killed in the battle of Cold Harbor during the Civil War. Companies B and C of the Sixth Infantry were the first troops to garrison this post on June 14, 1872.

On May 7, 1873, about one hundred Sioux attacked Ft. McKeen, which was then garrisoned by Companies B and C, Sixth Infantry and Co. H Seventh Infantry, commanded by Lieutenant Col. W.P. Carlin, Seventeenth Infantry.

June 15 and 17 Sioux Indians again made two separate attacks upon the post and were repulsed. Five times they gathered to attack, but each time they were beaten off.

So bold and frequent had been the attacks upon the military posts, escorts, working parties, and railroads in the Dept. of Dakota, that an additional regiment of cavalry, the Seventh, was transferred to that Dept. from the Military Division of the South for the purpose of following and punishing these Indians if they continued their attacks.

Accordingly, 6 additional cavalry quarters were built between the hill and river. Ft. McKeen received the name Ft. Abraham Lincoln by order of the Secretary of War, Nov. 19, 1872.

Ft. Lincoln was built across from the roistering town of Bismarck. Unlike older fortifications, it had no log stockade with loop-holed blockhouses at the corners; it was simply a collection of stables and barracks, the officers houses on higher ground. There were no trees in

FT. ABRAHAM LINCOLN—DAKOTA TERRITORY 1876. The Dakota column of the Yellowstone Expedition left the fort on May 17, 1876, looking for hostiles. The Seventh Cavalry under the command of Lt. Col. Custer, was the main element. Courtesy of the Custer Battlefield Museum.

FORT ABRAHAM LINCOLN as seen from the ferry boat landing on the east side of the Missouri River in the vicinity of Whiskey Point. Photo by Degraff. Courtesy of the North Dakota State Historical Society.

sight, but a few cottonwood whips being nursed along by the soldiers. The drinking water was the gritty stuff dipped from the Missouri.

All the buildings were built of pine lumber and plastered, with the exception of the stables and storehouses. The sawmill and shops were built of cottonwood. The quartermaster's stores, etc. were furnished from a depot at Jeffersonville, Indiana. Subsistence stores were sent from Chicago and Sioux City. Beef, hay and wood were supplied by contract. The area of the military reservation was 23½ square miles.

Ft. Lincoln's armament consisted of one 3-inch rifled, one 12-pdr mountain howitzer, one 12-pdr bronze, one 1-inch gatling and one ½-inch gatling.

Today the site of Ft. Abraham Lincoln is surrounded, except on the river front, by ravines, broken and irregular bluffs and hills. To the west and south are the "badlands". Land is generally sterile, soil light, gravelly, alkaline and very dry. The average rainfall is 13 inches. Timber is found in very limited quantities and is found mainly on the islands in the Missouri River and in the ravines. It consists mainly of cottonwood, elm, ash and oak.

The Sioux were an ever-present threat, but their depredations, as well as those of white thieves, were less of a nuisance and feared less than the mosquitos. Netting and smoke fires were necessary to human survival and even on blistering days, windows and doors had to be closed. Some cattle and horses, unable to endure the torture, were driven mad and died of exhaustion from fighting the pests which attacked them in shadowy clouds. Whimpering dogs sought relief in holes they dug into the sides of prairie swells. Fort Abraham Lincoln, said veteran cavalrymen, was the worst place on all the western plains for mosquitos.

Mrs. George A. Custer said of mosquitos: "I can see now how we women looked, taking our evening stroll: a little procession of fluttering females, with scarfs and over-dresses drawn over our heads, whisking handkerchiefs and beating the air with fans.

"We were obliged to make special toilets for our protection, and they were far from picturesque or becom-

BLOCKHOUSE AT FORT McKEEN used for protection as well as tedious guard duty. Courtesy of the Custer Battlefield Museum.

CAPT. CHARLES DeRUDIO AND DAUGHTERS. Photo by Barry. Courtesy of the Douglas County Historical Museum.

ing. Someone discovered that wrapping newspapers around our ankles and feet, and drawing the stocking over, would protect down to the slipper; then after tucking our skirts closely around us, we fixed ourselves in a chair, not daring to move.''

In 1874 Custer and the Seventh Cavalry were ordered by General Sheridan to conduct a reconnaissance of the Black Hills with the objective, among others, of opening a military road between Fort Abraham Lincoln and Fort Laramie.

The reconnaissance was eminently successful; the country of the Black Hills was found to contain plenty of fine timber, good soil, and an abundance of water and grass. Gold was also discovered by the expedition, leading to a subsequent rush of miners and others who were with difficulty restrained from a general invasion of the hills.

The barracks of the soldiers were on the side of the parade ground nearest the river, while seven detached houses for officers faced the river opposite. On the left of the parade ground was the long granary and the little military prison, called the guard house, opposite. Completing the square were the quartermaster and commissary storehouses for supplies and the adjutant's office. Outside the garrison proper, near the river were the stables for six hundred horses. Still farther beyond were the quarters for the laundresses, easily traced by their swinging clothes lines in front and dubbed for this reason ''suds row''. Some distance on from there were the log huts of the Indian scouts and their families, while on the same side also was the level plain used for parades and drill. On the left of the post was the sutler's store, with a billiard room attached. A citizen was permitted to put up a barber shop and later another built a little cabin of cottonwood with a canvas roof for a photographer's establishment. This was built by Goff in 1873. Barry later used it while staying at Ft. Lincoln to take photographs.

During the summer, the companies would live in pup tents some distance below the winter garrison. A private described the soldiers as he came to Ft. Lincoln in 1876: ''I was amazed and depressed, with the appearance of the camp. My patriotism went below zero as I saw how

FT. ABRAHAM LINCOLN 1885 showing Ft. Lincoln under its winter blanket. Photo by Barry. In the author's collection.

unkept the soldiers were—unshaved; uniforms flayed and dirty; many with their hair nearly down to their collars; gaunt and hungry looking, yet, as good and jolly a lot of men as I ever met. A hearty welcome was given us recruits, what a difference between the real soldiers we now met and those paper collar dudes at Ft. Snelling.

"Sure these Seventh Cavalry vets laugh at our blunders and have fun at our expense, but if you are in need of anything they have, you can have it for the asking; and if you want a friend who will stand by you through thick and thin, they are the boys to tie to.

"One tobacco-chewing trooper said, 'It is a good plan to feed up to the limit when you can, for you will need a hump like a camel to draw on when you get in the field.'

"I was assigned to one of the pup tents, with two other men. We were soon settled and ready for callers. The vets all wanted to know what was going on in the outside world.

"The pup tents are made of four pieces of canvas, the sections buttoned together with a short stake at each end and a ridge piece. The tent, in position, is only about three feet high and four feet long. You enter at one end, that is you crawl in, and you have to stay crawled until you come out. Pup tents are good to keep the sun off, but not much protection when it rains."

The soldiers received permission to put up a place in which they could have entertainments. They prepared the lumber in the sawmill. It was an ungainly looking structure, but large enough to hold them all. The unseasoned cottonwood warped even while the house was being built, but by patching and lining with old torn tents, they managed to keep out the storm. The scenery was painted on condemned canvas stretched on a framework, and was lifted off and on as the plays required. The foot lights in front of the rude stage were tallow candles that smoked and sputtered inside the clumsily cobbled casing of tin. The seats were narrow benches, without backs.

In 1874 the enlisted men organized a Fort Lincoln Dramatic Association. On one occasion, an amateur minstrel troop of soldiers from Fort Rice entertained the soldiers and officers at Fort Lincoln. Holidays such as

RUINS OF FT. McKEEN 1975. Photo by Bob Heski.

CURLEY, Crow Scout with Custer. Photo by Barry. Courtesy of
the Douglas County Historical Museum.

CAPTAIN THOMAS M. McDOUGALL. In the Little Big Horn fight, McDougall had the misfortune to command the regiment's pack train. In a letter to Barry, McDougall said of the Indians "Poor human fellows. They did what all of us would have done, so I long ago forgave them from the bottom of my heart. It won't be many years before you and I, Barry, must follow the same trail to the happy hunting grounds, and may we all pitch camp together." Photo by Barry. In the author's collection.

the Fourth of July and Christmas were appropriately observed.

On May 17, 1876, the Dakota Column left Fort Lincoln headed toward the Yellowstone which culminated in the disastrous Custer fight on June 25, 1876, on the banks of the Little Big Horn River.

Chief Joseph and his Nez Perce were forced to surrender on Oct. 5, 1877, after he had in 11 weeks moved his tribe 1,600 miles, engaged 10 separate U.S. commands in 13 battles and skirmishes, and in nearly every instance had either defeated them or fought them to a standstill. They were sent to Ft. Lincoln in flatboats and by wagon train arriving on Nov. 16, 1877.

The citizens of Bismarck organized a celebration to honor Colonel Miles, his escort, and Chief Joseph on the evening of November 19.

"The little city was on the 'buzz' getting ready to give a grand ball and supper in honor of Chief Joseph. The ladies of the fort joined in. There were no printed tickets. The tickets were $10.00 gold coin, ladies free and open to all."

A special banquet was also held in honor of Chief Joseph and two of his sub-chiefs. The invitation appeared in the Bismarck Tri-Weekly on Nov. 21, 1877:

"To Joseph, Head Chief of the Nez Perces.

Sir:

Desiring to show you our kind feelings and admiration we have for your bravery and humanity, as exhibited in your recent conflict with the forces of the United States, we most cordially invite you to dine with us at the Sheridan House in this city. The dinner to be given at 1½ p.m. today." After all the honors and banquets, Joseph and his band were placed on a train and headed for Ft. Leavenworth to await the judgement of the government.

For several years following the Battle of the Little Big Horn, the post was very active. In the fall of 1876, General Alfred Terry, after returning from the Little Big Horn expedition, organized a force of about 1,200 men at Fort Lincoln, and proceeded to disarm the Indians in the various agencies on the river and confiscate their ponies.

After work was renewed on the Northern Pacific

MAJOR MARCUS RENO, second in command of the Seventh Cavalry at the Battle of the Little Big Horn. He was sent by Custer to attack the village. Forced to go on the defensive, he led a retreat from the river bottom and by doing so possibly saved his men from Custer's fate. Photo by Barry. In the author's collection.

Railroad in 1879, Fort Lincoln gave protection to the various surveying and construction parties. During the middle eighties, the fort declined rapidly. In 1889, the ordinance depot which had been established at the fort in 1878 was removed to Ft. Snelling, Minnesota. The post was ordered to be discontinued July 22, 1891, and was abandoned a month later. On October 15, Fort Lincoln Military Reservation, comprising 24,800 acres was turned over to the Dept. of Interior for disposal.

Following the abandonment, the buildings of the post were placed under the charge of a custodian. Several unsuccessful attempts were made by the state to use the buildings. On Dec. 1, 1894, a small army of about 100 men equipped with tools and 60 teams arrived and dismantled the buildings. Only three buildings remained. These were sold at public auctions.

Somewhere in and around Bismarck and Mandan may exist parts of old Fort Lincoln, once the most important post in the states. Today, there isn't much left. Maybe someday, they will again rebuild her as a memorial to those that served her, so that her name doesn't fade away in the now dusty pages of history.

REMAINS OF CUSTER'S HOME 1975. Photo by Bob Heski.

CHAPTER SEVEN
SENTINEL AND GUARDIAN

FORTS BUFORD AND YATES

Fort Buford stands on the north bank of the Missouri River at the point where the Yellowstone River empties into the Missouri River from the south.

The site of the fort was chosen by General Alfred Sully during the 1864 campaign against the Sioux Indians. It was the first military post built in this portion of Dakota Territory. Those previously built were fur company trading posts.

The discovery of gold in Montana and Idaho in the early 1860's made it necessary to keep the Missouri River open to navigation. In order to do this, military posts were built. These posts included forts Stevenson, Buford, Shaw, Benton and Camp Cooke.

Captain W. G. Rankin and "C" Company of the 13th Infantry with only a few axes and tools were sent to construct this post June 15, 1866. The "lonesome seventy" were attacked the second night, suffered a casualty and almost lost their cattle herd.

Captain Rankin contracted for the old Fort Union Fur Post and tore it down and used much of the lumber to build Ft. Buford.

The men were not carpenters or masons, and most weren't good soldiers, but they did their best with what they had. Their first winter on the high plains must have been one of absolute misery.

They built their barracks walls of adobe and cottonwood, and made the roofs of cottonwood slabs and sod. The use of mud for building was unsatisfactory because it would dissolve quite readily. With each thaw and freeze, the cottonwood timbers would expand and contract causing gaps to appear and the sod roofs continually dripped water.

The Fort Buford military reservation was declared by President Andrew Johnson on August 18, 1868. It had a total area of about thirty square miles. In 1870 this was reduced.

The surrounding country was not suitable for plowing. It was poorly watered. The soil was alkaline. The principle timber consisted of cottonwood, which made inferior lumber. The climate varied, the heat of summer was short and the nights generally cool. Winter usually lasted from December until April.

Quartermaster and subsistence stores were furnished from depots at Chicago, Illinois; St. Louis, Missouri; Leavenworth, Kansas; and Jeffersonville, Indiana. Wood was furnished by contract and the water was obtained from the Missouri River by wagon.

The armament of Ft. Buford consisted of one 3 inch rifle, two bronze 12 pdrs, and two iron and bronze 6 pdrs.

Many times officers and men alike would turn to drink in order to attain a "happy median". Ft. Buford had two post commanders that would frequently indulge. They were Capt. Rankin and Lt. Col. Bowman.

Later on in 1874, holiday inebriation was taken more or less for granted at Ft. Buford. The post surgeon entered the following in his record of events for Dec. 25, 1874.

"Christmas day was very quiet. The companies had a very nice dinner and were presented with three gallons each of whisky by the post trader."

During the 1887 hunt for Chief Joseph and his Nez Perce, the Seventh Cavalry stopped at the fort and it was said: "Ft. Buford is a large post situated nearly opposite the point where the Yellowstone River enters the Missouri. It is garrisoned by five infantry companies and countless mosquitos. Our men are in all good spirits and the sutler at Ft. Buford is having a big trade. The demand for rattlesnake poison is brisk."

After Chief Joseph and his band of Nez Perce surrendered, they were brought to Fort Buford. Steamboats weren't available that late in the year, so Joseph and much of his band were sent down river to Bismarck in flatboats. The rest of Joseph's band were sent in wagons.

On Nov. 9, special order No. 225 directed the release of five companies from Ft. Buford to escort the Nez Perce prisoners to Bismarck. The operators of the flatboats were offered high wages to undertake the Missouri River trip down river. Speed was important, because the slush was turning into ice blocks on the river. Only one flatboat was lost, with a few Indian lives.

In 1885 there were approximately four hundred people living around Fort Buford, three-fourths of that number belonged to the army. Among the others were eleven farmers, two wood dealers, one lawyer, druggist, bookkeeper, beggar, post trader, interpreter, saddler, wheelwright, and one bartender, two laborers, four railroad workers and cooks, twenty-five teamsters, ten wood choppers, two herders, twenty-seven musicians and two blacksmiths.

In 1895 Ft. Buford was abandoned and a year later the buildings were sold at public auction.

So ended the life at Ft. Buford, sentinel of the Missouri.

OFFICER'S ROW, FT. BUFORD, D. T. Major Brotherton's quarters are believed to be on the right. From 1878-1890 Barry visited Ft. Buford. From about 1880-1883 he brought his portable gallery with him. He spent many nights at officer's row. While visiting the post, he came in personal contact with Col. Partello, Lt. Liggett, Generals Slocum and Miles, and Maj. Brotherton, as well as numerous soldiers, Indians and traders that visited the fort. It was Maj. Brotherton that gave Barry permission to take Gall's photograph with the warning — don't cause trouble. Courtesy of the Custer Battlefield Museum.

FORT BUFORD, NORTH DAKOTA, looking northwest. As time went by, Ft. Buford had seven sets of barracks built of adobe on stone foundations. It had 19 sets of officers quarters on stone foundations with frame and horizontal siding, lathed and plastered on the inside. It also consisted of a hospital, guard house, six storehouses, a bakery, two corrals with stables, quartermaster's office, adjutant's office, laundress' quarters, library and a school. Later a gymnasium and a bowling alley were added. Courtesy of the North Dakota State Histocial Society.

STANDING ROCK AGENCY—FT. YATES

After the Teton Sioux surrendered, some of the government officials wanted all of the Tetons to be sent to Indian territory; others, however, wanted to establish agencies for them along the Missouri River. After strong protests by Red Cloud and Spotted Tail, a compromise was eventually reached. Red Cloud's Oglalas were settled in the southwest corner of the reservation at Pine Ridge. To the east of Pine Ridge, Spotted Tail and his Brule's were settled along the Little White River. Their agency was called Rosebud. The remaining Sioux tribes were settled on Lower Brule', Crow Creek, Cheyenne River, and Standing Rock.

D. F. Barry spent a lot of time at Fort Yates taking photographs, as well as at other agencies. Although he didn't have a gallery there, he did have quarters there. He became a good friend of Gall, Sitting Bull and other notable Sioux, as well as Agent McLaughlin.

In 1882, Governor Newton Evans, Judge Peter C. Shannon, and James H. Teller attempted to secure an agreement with the Sioux for the purpose of cutting up the Great Sioux reservation into separate ones, attached to the various agencies and opening some 14,000 square miles of Indian lands to sale and settlement. This ended in failure because of the arousal of public sentiment and the position of some members of the Senate and administration.

1883 marked another try at breaking up Indian lands. Senator Henry L. Dawes, Senator John Logan, Angus Cameron, John Morgan and George Vest looked extensively into conditions among the Sioux and found that the people were opposed to the agreements proposed. This put a stop to further attempts of this sort.

In 1888 Capt. R. H. Pratt, Judge John Wright and Rev. William J. Cleveland were sent by the government with a "new deal." They wanted to offer the Sioux 50¢ per acre for the cession of lands west of the 102nd degree of west longitude and between the Cheyenne and White Rivers. These lands would be added to the public domain. The money would be given to the Sioux nation. A fund of one million dolars was to be set aside at once for the education of Indians in agriculture, and for other

SUMMER CAMP OF TROOPS AT FORT BUFORD 1875. When winter was over, the troops would bivouac outside the confines of the fort and begin drilling to rid themselves of the laziness, sluggishness and partially neglected and forgotten skills that often accompanied winter soldiering. Photo by A. C. Leighton. Courtesy of the North Dakota State Historical Society.

MOUNTED TROOPS OF THE SEVENTH CAVALRY AT FORT YATES. In 1878, Ft. Yates was officially designated to guard not only Standing Rock Agency, but also Grand River Agency. Fort Rice, protector of Grand River Agency and the first post on the Missouri, was phased out in 1878. In the late 1870's and early 1880's the army made an increased effort to curtail drinking. As a result a considerable amount of hard liquor was smuggled into the post. The surgeon at Fort Yates complained that the soldiers, as a result of prohibition, were purchasing and drinking extracts of lemon, vanilla, cinnamon, peppermint, ginger, worcestershire, and red pepper sauces, bay rum, cologne and many medicines containing large percentages of alcohol. Photo by Barry. Courtesy of the Denver Public Library, Western History Dept.

FT. YATES, D. T. Ft. Yates and the Agency were built back on a ridge which, rising above the bottom lands and the river, forms a broad, level table upon which are the buildings, stores, warehouses, school houses, churches and offices. The first school at Standing Rock was organized and taught by Louise Van Solen. The first mission school was run by Bishop Marty. The Standing Rock Mission of "St. Elizabeth" was given $5,000 by John J. Astor to carry on its work. The Catholic Mission was later run by Fathers Martin and Christostum. Mrs. Barry patiently waits in the wagon. Photo by Barry. Courtesy of the Custer Battlefield Museum.

STANDING ROCK AGENCY. The Agency was established by Executive Order on April 12, 1870. It contained the upper and lower Yanktonnais, Hunkpapa and Blackfoot Sioux with a population of 7,322. Photo by Barry. Courtesy of the Denver Public Library, Western History Dept.

purposes. Twenty-five thousand cows and one thousand bulls were to be purchased for distribution. They failed to obtain the required signatures and they gave up.

McLaughlin said, "The agreement proposed was not the sort of proposition I would make to a friend of mine, but the people who were pressing it, did not regard the Indian in the light of a friend."

Since "those people" paid McLaughlin's salary he didn't do much of anything against it.

Gen. Crook, senators Charles Foster and William Warner were delegated to carry another deal to the Sioux, only this time they offered the Sioux $1.50 an acre.

They visited Rosebud, Pine Ridge, Lower Brule', Crow Creek, and Cheyenne River Agencies. They needed ¾ of the adult male signatures. On July 27 they arrived at Standing Rock Agency. Here the decision was to be made.

The Hunkpapas and Blackfoot refused to sign. Crook asked for McLaughlin's help. McLaughlin held secret meetings with John Grass until he agreed to speak for its ratification and work for it.

On Aug. 3, 1889, a final agreement was held with the commissioners. McLaughlin didn't inform Sitting Bull about the meeting. He arrived just as the signing was almost complete. After the signing, a newspaperman asked Sitting Bull how the Indians felt about giving up their lands. "Indians!" Sitting Bull shouted. "There are no Indians left but me!"

McLaughlin had employed all his influences to bring the leading Sioux around. Most of the squawmen and mixed bloods were openly working for the commission.

The Ghost Dance craze spread to all of the Indian agencies. When Kicking Bear, a Minneconju Sioux, appeared and described the new religion of the Ghost Dance, Sitting Bull listened with some skepticism. He invited Kicking Bear to remain at Standing Rock and teach them the Dance of the Ghosts.

McLaughlin sent a police force to eject him from Standing Rock. The first group of Indian police wouldn't do it so McLaughlin sent a larger force. McLaughlin viewed the Ghost Dance as a personal threat to his posi-

SITTING BULL'S TRIAL AT STANDING ROCK AGENCY FOR INSTIGATING THE CROWS TO GO ON THE WAR PATH; 1886. Sitting Bull is seen front center of the photograph. Three men at the table are left to right: Col. Townsend, 12th Infantry; Col. Barrister (grey hat); and Indian Commissioner James McLaughlin. McLaughlin was appointed Oct. 27, 1881, to "run" Standing Rock Agency by President Chester A. Arthur. He first met Sitting Bull on Sept. 8, 1881, and said, "he is a stocky man with an evil face and shifty eyes, desirous of making friends". McLaughlin fostered a rift between Sitting Bull, Gall and other chiefs. He was willing to use any Indian he could to effectively combat the influence of Sitting Bull. If anything went wrong on Standing Rock, McLaughlin blamed Sitting Bull personally. Photo by Barry, 1886. Courtesy of the Smithsonian Institution, National Anthropological Archives, Bureau of American Ethnology Collection.

tion and the smooth-running system he had created at the agency. Therefore, to rid himself of this new threat, he notified the Commissioner of Indian Affairs of conditions at Standing Rock and added that the real power behind the problem was Sitting Bull.

On Dec. 12, 1890, Lt. Col. Wm. F. Drum, commanding troops at Fort Yates received an order to arrest Sitting Bull. On Dec. 15, 1890, forty-three Indian policeman surrounded Sitting Bull's cabin on Grand River and tried to arrest him. A fight between Sitting Bull's followers ensued and Sitting Bull among others was killed. McLaughlin at last had his wish to get Sitting Bull out of the way.

The Indians by the hundreds fled from Standing Rock, seeking refuge in the Ghost Dance camps or with the last of the great chiefs. About a hundred of these fleeing Hunkpapas reached Big Foot's Minneconju Camp, which unknowingly lead to Wounded Knee.

In 1903 Fort Yates was abandoned by the military. The buildings gradually fell into a state of disrepair. The only one guarding it now was the ghost of Sitting Bull.

INDIAN COUNCIL AT FORT YATES. The politicians preferred to force the Indians into selling a large portion of their reservation out of fear that it would be taken from them if they failed to sell. If it worked, the government wouldn't have to break the treaty. Photo by Barry. Courtesy of the Douglas County Historical Museum.

TATANKA YOTANKA (SITTING BULL) surrendered in 1881 and was turned over to Mr. J. A. Stephan, the agent at Standing Rock Agency. Instead of sending Sitting Bull to the Hunkpapa Agency at Standing Rock, the government again broke its promise to give him a pardon and sent him to Fort Randall as a military prisoner for 2 years. In an interview he said, "If the Great Father gives me a reservation, I do not want to be confined to any part of it. I want no restraint. I will keep on the reservation, but I want to go where I please. I don't want a whiteman over me. I don't want an agent. I will keep the whiteman with me, but not as my chief. I ask this because I want to do right by my people. I cannot trust anyone else to trade with them or talk to them." Photo by Barry. Courtesy of the Douglas County Historical Museum.

69

GUARD MOUNT AT FORT YATES, D. T. The military post adjacent to the Agency was established on June 6, 1875. Its primary function was to police Standing Rock Agency. Fort Yates consisted of barracks and laundress' quarters, two sets of officer's quarters, two storehouses, a hospital and bakery, quartermaster's stables and additional buildings. The quartermaster and subsistence stores were furnished from depots at Jeffersonville, Indiana, and Chicago, Illinois, via Sioux City and Bismarck. Photo by Barry. Courtesy of the Douglas County Historical Museum.

THE 2ND SIOUX COMMISSION 1888 appointed by President Cleveland to further break up the Great Sioux Reserve. (left to right) Rev. William J. Cleveland; Judge John V. Wright of Tennessee; and Capt. Richard Henry Pratt, Chairman of the Commission.

Photo by Barry. Courtesy of the Smithsonian Institution, National Anthropological Archives, Bureau of American Ethnology Collection.

RAIN-IN-THE-FACE, HUNKPAPA DAKOTA. In 1874, Rain-in-the-Face was taken from Standing Rock Agency by the Seventh Cavalry and imprisoned at Fort Lincoln for supposedly killing two whites in 1873. He subsequently escaped and later met the Custers again at the Little Big Horn. Photo by Barry. Courtesy of the Smithsonian Institution, National Anthropological Archives, Bureau of American Ethnology Collection.

THROWING STICK, Dakota Sioux. Photo by Barry. Courtesy of the Smithsonian Institution, National Anthropological Archives, Bureau of American Ethnology Collection.

PIZI (CHIEF GALL) AND HIS NEPHEW, Hunkpapa Sioux. Photo by Barry. Courtesy of the Smithsonian Institution, National Anthropological Archives, Bureau of American Ethnology Collection.

GOOD HORSE AND FAMILY. Photo by Barry. Courtesy of the Smithsonian Institution, National Anthropological Archives, Bureau of American Ethnology Collection.

RATION DAY AT STANDING ROCK AGENCY. Semi-monthly on ration day, the different bands of Sioux headed to Standing Rock Agency for their rations. They would come on ponies, foot and driving teams filled to overflowing with women, children and men with all of their belongings. The cattle were killed and butchered in the corral, and the allowance of meat and other articles was allotted to the head of each family. The Indians would spend two or three days visiting, dancing and feasting; then head back to their allotted lands the way they came. Photo by Barry. In the author's collection.

CHIEF RED FISH AND SONS. Photo by Barry. In the author's collection.

SLOW WHITE BUFFALO, CROW EAGLE, IRON THUNDER AND FOOL THUNDER, Dakota Sioux. Photo by Barry. Courtesy of the Smithsonian Institution, National Anthropological Archives, Bureau of American Ethnology Collection.

LT. BULL HEAD. In charge of the Indian police. Sent by Agent McLaughlin to arrest Sitting Bull on Dec. 15, 1890. He was shot by one of Sitting Bull's followers. As he fell, he accidently shot Sitting Bull. Photo by Barry. Courtesy of the Douglas County Historical Museum.

RED CLOUD. "The Hostile of his time". Photo by Barry. Courtesy of the Douglas County Historical Museum.

GOOSE, DAKOTA SIOUX. Photo by Barry. Courtesy of the Smithsonian Institution, National Anthropological Archives, Bureau of American Ethnology Collection.

CHIEF LONG DOG. Photo by Barry. Courtesy of the Douglas County Historical Museum.

CHIEF YOUNG-MAN-AFRAID-OF-HIS-HORSES. Chief of the Oglala Sioux, contemporaneous with Red Cloud and one of the leading lieutenants of the latter in the war of 1866 to defeat the building of the Montana road through the buffalo pastures of Powder River. Photo by Barry. In the author's collection.

BOB BRAVE BEAR, a sort of Indian dude. He and an associate "The Only One" killed and robbed a settler near Pembina, North Dakota, in 1873. He was put in jail in Pembina but escaped, killed a man and fled to Canada where he joined Sitting Bull. He surrendered with Sitting Bull in 1881. He was condemned and hanged. Photo by Barry. Courtesy of the Douglas County Historical Museum.

GENERAL FARIBAULT AND CHIEF JOHN GRASS. Photo by Barry. Courtesy of the Douglas County Historical Museum.

CHIEF MAD BEAR. Photo by Barry. Courtesy of the Douglas County Historical Museum.

RAIN-IN-THE-FACE AT FT. YATES on his favorite pony. Rain-in-the-Face asked Barry if he would get him an audience with Governor John Miller of North Dakota. He wanted his friend Barry to intercede to the Governor and make him a policeman at the State Capital. Governor Miller agreed, but then asked if Rain-in-the-Face could speak English. When Barry told him no, his application was rejected. He later learned a few English words and became an Indian policeman as the Indians settled down to the yoke of reservation life. Courtesy of the Douglas County Historical Museum.

INDIAN DANCERS AT STANDING ROCK AGENCY. Photo by
Barry. In the author's collection.

STEPS, brother of Chief Joseph. He was found in a snowstorm by the Sioux and subsequently moved to Standing Rock Agency. Photo by Barry. Courtesy of the Smithsonian Institution, National Anthropological Archives, Bureau of American Ethnology Collection.

STANDING ROCK AGENCY (Ft. Yates, D.T.) The building with the "X" is the trader's store where the young Sioux Chief Rain-in-the-Face was captured by a detail under the command of Tom Custer and transported to the Ft. Lincoln guard house. Inset photo is of Captain George Yates. Standing Rock Agency was later changed to Ft. Yates in honor of this officer who was killed with Custer. Photo by Barry. Courtesy of the Custer Battlefield Museum.

CHIEF RED HORSE, one of Sitting Bull's followers, was digging wild turnips with some women when Custer attacked. He later drew a large number of pictographs about the battle. Photo by Barry. In the author's collection.

STEAMER F. Y. BATCHELOR AT THE FORT BUFORD LANDING 1878. Ft. Buford was important as a relay point for both freight and passengers coming up river on steamboats. Steamboats could usually get this far even though the Yellowstone was too low to continue further.. The arrival of a steamboat was a momentous occasion since it brought news from civilization. There were strange faces to see and talk with as well as mail from home. Months were spent waiting for the steamboats. Enlisted men quickly became masters of trading with the boats' roustabouts for anything the army called contraband. Courtesy of the North Dakota State Historical Society.

SITTING BULL'S GRAVE, Ft. Yates, North Dakota. Shows the location where Sitting Bull's battered remains were buried in quicklime. It is rumored that Sitting Bull's body was removed to a new location on the Grand River near the town of Mobridge, South Dakota, where a large monument was placed. Photo by the author.

ONE BULL, nephew of Sitting Bull, with his wife and child outside their home on the reservation. Many Indians would rather sleep in their tipis than in the houses provided for them. Photo by Barry.

Courtesy of the Smithsonian Institution, National Anthropological Archives, Bureau of American Ethnology Collection.

CHAPTER EIGHT
INDEPENDENT PHOTOGRAPHER 1884-1890

The summer of 1883 found Barry at Fort Custer, Montana. During the summer, he also traveled to the Custer Battlefield and took various photographs. During his sojurn at Ft. Custer his portable pre-fabricated gallery was carried away by a windstorm and never seen again.

After Barry returned from Ft. Custer, he rested in Bismarck and decided to take an extended trip east. He left on Oct. 18th.

When he took over Goff's gallery in the spring of 1884, Barry stayed pretty close to Bismarck, although he did tour the forts and agencies. Occasionally he would take his wife along; she was the attractive Margaret (Patti) Young whom he married in March of 1884.

On May 16, 1884, the Bismarck Tribune advertised the following:

"Barry's photograph parlors. The rooms formerly occupied by O. S. Goff have been handsomely furnished by Mr. D. F. Barry who is now prepared to furnish photographs of all sizes and styles, shades and character. The rooms are unquestionably the finest on the line of the Northern Pacific road, and the facilities for taking pictures are as good as is possible to obtain. The reception room is a model of beauty and neatness and has an appearance at once inviting the pleasant. Mr. Barry has just received the largest sized camera and can take a life-sized photograph or large groups, which will be appreciated especially by those who desire family groups or life-sized photos. A specialty will be made of children's pictures taken by the instantaneous process, so that the "beauty of the baby" can be transferred to paper between the laughs and cries. The latest novelties in the photographic line include panels of all sizes and shades. Mr. Barry's reputation as a photographer is sufficient guarantee of the excellence of his work."

Barry after taking over Goff's studio in 1884, could take photographs by the instantaneous process due to the large skylight in the studio. He advertised the process as well as children's pictures, a specialty.

"If there is anytime when a person is good looking, it is when surrounded by all that is beautiful and attractive, and the scenic effects, backgrounds and general surroundings of this magnificient new gallery cannot but inspire one to at least a pleasant expression. No better photography can be made in Chicago or New York, and Bismarck can truthfully boast of as complete and elegantly arrayed a gallery as can be found in the largest cities. Call on Mr. Barry and take a glimpse of his palatial rooms."

Bismarck in 1884 had a population of about 5,032. Barry toured many of the forts such as Lincoln, Buford and Standing Rock Agency. Most of the people around these forts and agencies consisted mainly of the military.

As Barry visited the different posts and agencies, he became a favorite among most of the people he met. This friendship encompassed officers and men, Indians and many notable and influential people. He liked to play poker and played with anyone who liked the game. He was a great conversationalist and enjoyed being with people.

John Mulvaney the artist of "Custer's Last Rally" was a friend of Barry's.

In 1885 Barry photographed Fort Lincoln from the bluff adjoining Fort McKeen. He also took photographs of various buildings at Fort Lincoln, among them General Custer's old house. During 1885, he photographed Chief Gall, John Grass and Rain-in-the-Face and added them to his collection.

"Sitting Bull almost had a mania for having his picture made in later years. He was never much adverse to it, but always had to be paid for his troubles. He would take almost anything as a gift, until Buffalo Bill took him away with his show. That ruined him, for he found he could sell his pictures."

Mr. Barry was called Icastinyanka Cikala Hanzi "Catcher, Little Shadow" by the Indians. He was only about five feet five inches tall and was believed to be, by the Indians, a medicine man who could transplant the human body on a piece of paper.

Barry's pictures were reproduced in almost all of the leading magazines, newspapers and in countless books. Had it not been for many of his photographs, history would have to rely solely on word pictures of many of the Indians. His photographs were the only ones ever taken of some of the historically prominent Indians, and many were taken under spartan and dangerous conditions.

The year of 1886 had many thinking of the Custer Battle that occurred a scant ten years previously. Many of the survivors of the battle decided to return to the battlefield to commemorate the tragic event.

Gall went along to give the first accurate description of the battle. Reticent at first, he finally told his story with dignity and animation.

Captain Godfrey was in charge of the arrangements. Capt. Baldwin with men of Company "K" Fifth Infantry, served as escort to the group. Other members attending included Major Benteen, Captains McDougall and Edgerly, Lts. Slocum and Mann and Sgt. Hall and

D. F. BARRY, the young businessman. A self photograph. Courtesy of the Denver Public Library, Western History Dept.

PATTI BARRY. Barry returned from Quincy, Ill. with his bride, the former Margaret Young (Patti). She was born April 1, 1864, in New Orleans where her parents were spending the winter. Their home was in Quincy, Illinois. She married Mr. Barry in March of 1884. Mrs. Barry enjoyed traveling occasionally with her husband. Photo by Barry, March of 1888. Courtesy of Mr. and Mrs. Vernon Barry.

MAIN STREET, BISMARCK 1889. Constitutional Convention Parade. Courtesy of the North Dakota State Historical Society.

Trumpeter Penwell. Colonel Cochran and Lt. Partello of the Fifth Infantry were also in attendance along with a delegation of officers and ladies from Fort Custer.

Barry returned in July to Bismarck with Dr. Porter after the reunion. Barry, Partello, and Godfrey visited Custer Battlefield on June 25, 1886, June 25, 1899, and June 25, 1926. Sitting Bull and Rain-in-the-Face met at Barry's gallery at Standing Rock and wanted to know what had taken place at the battlefield.

Barry through his photography helped many photographers and artists.

H. H. Cross, a famous Chicago painter of Indians sent Barry a painting of Chief Gall in appreciation of the assistance he rendered the painter by furnishing him with photographs and other materials for his work. Mr. Cross painted most of the Indian paintings which were contained in the Walker collection at Chicago. He also painted a large number of famous race horses. Barry put the painting in his studio among his collection of Indian photographs and relics.

Barry sent photographs of Indians to Mr. Landry of Cincinnati who used them to paint his conception of "Hiawatha appearing from the Woodland." The painting took first place at the National Photographers' Convention where competition encompassed the world. Mr. Landry sent Barry the painting in appreciation for his help. He also sent the photographer large photographs of Booth and Barrett which became famous in art circles.

Photographers adapted their style and approach to conform to the prevailing taste for elaborate and artistic decor. The use of painted background and various accessories were commonplace in photographers' establishments all over America.

In 1887 at Fort Yates, North Dakota, General Godfrey, Barry and other Indian fighters were assembled at a poker game in Barry's quarters. Barry held four kings in his hand and boosted the game accordingly. The others dropped out until there were two of them left, Barry and Godfrey.

Barry raised by fives and larger sums, but Godfrey raised only a dollar at a time. Bidding continued until Barry became suspicious of his large raises and God-

STERNWHEELER ROSEBUD taken at Drowned Man's Rapids. Photo by Barry. Courtesy of the Douglas County Historical Museum.

PASS IN REVIEW. The frontier cavalry at its finest at Ft. Custer, Montana, 1887. O.S. Goff photo. Courtesy of the Custer Battlefield Museum.

RENO'S FIRST CROSSING 1886, looking toward the area where Reno first crossed and headed on line toward the Indian village.

Photo by Barry. Courtesy of the Douglas County Historical Museum.

CUSTER BATTLE RIDGE where Custer made his last stand. The inset is of Lt. Jack Sturgis who died with Custer, and whose body was never identified. Photo by Barry, inset by Goff. Courtesy of the Douglas County Historical Museum.

GENERAL JOHN GIBBON. He was in command of the Montana column from Fort Ellis in the Yellowstone Expedition of 1876. Photo by Barry. Courtesy of the Denver Public Library, Western History Dept.

DR. PORTER. The surviving surgeon of the Custer fight attached to the Reno command, joined a party from Fort Yates that was headed for Fort Custer for the 10th Anniversary of the Custer fight. He was joined by Captain Godfrey, Lt. Slocum, Chief Gall, Louis Sitting Bull and photographer D. F. Barry, who was asked to take photographs of the Battlefield and surroundings. Photo by Barry. Courtesy of the Denver Public Library, Western History Dept.

LT. CHARLES DeRUDIO. He became unhorsed in Reno's retreat from the valley and hid in the timber, later joining the command on the bluffs. Courtesy of the Douglas County Historical Museum.

BATTLEFIELD DEBRIS showing the horse bones, taken June 25, 1886. Photo by Barry. In the author's collection.

TENTH ANNIVERSARY SURVIVORS AT FORT CUSTER. No. 1 Capt. McDougal; 2. Capt. Benteen; 3. Col. Dudley; 4. Lt. Brewer; 5. Dr. Porter; 6. Lt. Mann; 7. Tingell of the St. Paul Globe; 8. Capt. Garrety; 9. Baker of the St. Paul Globe; 10. Capt. Godfrey; 11. Fred Benteen Jr.; 12. Col. Slocum; 13. Col. Partello. Photo by Barry. Courtesy of the Custer Battlefield Museum.

CAPTAIN F. W. BENTEEN. Custer sent him to the left to catch escaping hostiles. He returned in time to save Reno's troops. Barry was a friend, and they wrote to each other intermittently. Each agreed that neither would divulge the correspondence of the other.

After Benteen died in 1898, Barry burned most of the correspondence between them. Barry saved a few of the letters and broke silence by discussing parts of them. Photo by Barry. In the author's collection.

frey's minimal ones.

"Finally" Barry said, "I met his raise and threw my cards face downward on the table saying 'Mr. Godfrey has four aces' and sure enough, there were four aces in Godfrey's hand." This was just one of the amusing incidents Barry experienced.

An artist's sketch recalled the historic poker game at the frontier army post. Joe Schenerle, visiting Gen. Godfrey, sketched this scene from various accounts.

A second Sioux commission was established in 1888 by the government to further break up the Great Sioux Reserve.

Barry sent information on Rain-in-the-Face to Arthur Linn, a writer for the Sunday Tribune. He publicly thanked Barry and said he was under obligation to Capt. D. F. Barry of Bismarck, the noted photographer of Indian characters. Now Barry had a rank!

In November, Barry returned from Fort Yates. While on his visit, he acquired many photographs which he added to his rapidly growing collection.

Mrs. Barry's sister Mrs. Colonel Walcott of Quincy,

Illinois, died in Quincy in late November. The death was a severe blow to Mrs. Barry. Mr. Barry remained in Bismarck, while his wife went home.

Barry traveled to Grand River to visit Sitting Bull in 1889. He acquired a few photographs and had Sitting Bull write his autograph on the back of his calling card.

From the early 1890's onward, the capture of the "Fleeting moment" became a universally popular game. Many times Barry would use this theme in advertising his photographs.

The instantaneous process was used by Barry in the later 1880's and early 90's. It employed ordinary collodion and development, but required the best illumination possible. The negatives were frequently strengthened or intensified by mercuric chloride.

In 1890 Barry went east to Superior, Wisconsin, on a business trip. He liked what he saw and checked out the booming city for his photography business. He planned on leaving Bismarck, his decision prompted by the lack of interest in his photographs. A friend, Joseph Scanlon, later editor of the Miles City Star, told Barry that the area

CUSTER BATTLEFIELD looking toward the river before a general clean up of the battlefield. Notice the boot bottom affixed to a stake. The tops were cut off by the Indian women for moccasin soles. Courtesy of the Custer Battlefield Museum.

MONUMENT TO THE DEAD. Three granite blocks were hauled by teams from the bank of the Big Horn River in the summer of 1881. The work was completed on July 29, 1881. Photo by Barry, around the time the memorial was completed. Courtesy of the Douglas County Historical Museum.

THE RIDGE where Custer and his men dismounted and fought, as told by Chief Gall on the 10th Anniversary, June 25, 1886. Captain Frank D. Baldwin's Company K, Fifth Infantry was photographed where Custer dismounted. Photo by Barry. Courtesy of the Douglas County Historical Museum.

LOOKING TOWARD THE BLUFFS Reno's command climbed after their retreat from the timber. Photo by Barry on the 10th Anniversary of the Battle.

RENO HILL 1886. Mr. Barry in his travels around the Custer Battlefield took many photographs from Reno's crossing to the bluffs across the Little Big Horn where Reno made his final entrenchment position. He also photographed Custer hill. In his travels on the field, he found a watch, overlooked by the Indians, as well as a finger bone. While taking one photograph, he had to abandon his position because of a rattlesnake. Photo by Barry. Courtesy of the Douglas County Historical Museum.

D. F. BARRY (RIGHT) AND SITTING BULL'S TWO WIVES AND DAUGHTERS with an unidentified white man. The reservation Indians were a peculiar people and for years had a superstitious dread of the camera. A dread that ironically was confined to the men; for the women didn't object to having their photographs taken. Photo by Barry. Courtesy of the Smithsonian Institution, National Anthropological Archives, Bureau of American Ethnology Collection.

CHIEF LONG SOLDIER. Photo by Barry. Courtesy of the Douglas County Historical Museum.

HAIRY CHIN dressed in an Uncle Sam costume. He led a fourth of July parade in Bismarck, North Dakota. Two days after he returned to the Standing Rock Agency, he died. The Indians claimed that dressing as Uncle Sam was bad medicine which therefore caused him to die. After that, no Sioux would parade as Uncle Sam. Photo by Barry 1889. Courtesy of the Smithsonian Institution, National Anthropological Archives, Bureau of American Ethnology Collection.

RAIN-IN-THE-FACE AND WIFE SATI. While hunting buffalo as a fugitive in Canada with Sitting Bull, his horse stumbled and fell with him discharging a pistol which wounded him in the knee. From then on he had to use a crutch because of a lame leg. Barry said, "Rain-in-the-Face was the most docile Indian that ever sat before my camera. He was always willing to pose, and had a ready palm for gifts. He was a great convenience to me in keeping down my stock of linen, for he also had a mania for white shirts." Photo by Barry. Courtesy of the Douglas County Historical Museum.

CHIEF GALL. He attended the Tenth Anniversary of the Custer fight and told his story of the fight. Photo by Barry. In the author's collection.

BLACK BULL known as a wag and a wit, carried a bundle of papers from various white men stating that he was a chief and deserved special consideration. He told the commission that if they wanted to buy Indian land, the Indians were willing to sell it at a fair price. He suggested that they bring in a big scale. The Indians would weigh the earth and sell it by the pound. Photo by Barry. Courtesy of the Douglas County Historical Museum.

SITTING BULL'S AUTOGRAPH. Barry traveled to Grand River to take Sitting Bull's photograph. While there, he took a few photographs and had Sitting Bull write his autograph on the backs of several cards. Courtesy of the Douglas County Historical Museum.

FORTUNATELY, BARRY apparently liked to experiment with photography by taking a number of pictures of himself. This self portrait is courtesy of the Denver Public Library, Western History Dept.

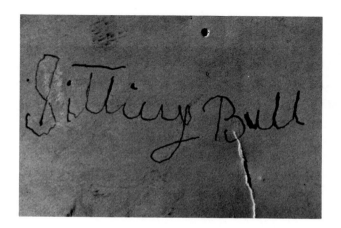

SITTING BULL'S LITTLE GIRL, STANDING HOLY. Photo by Barry. In the author's collection.

NORTH DAKOTA LEGISLATURE 1880'S. Photo by Barry. Courtesy of the Douglas County Historical Museum.

HIAWATHA APPEARING FROM THE WOODLAND. Barry sent photographs to Mr. Landry of Cincinnati who used them to paint his conception of "Hiawatha Appearing from the Woodland". The painting took first place at the National Photographers' Convention where competition encompassed the world. Mr. Landry sent Barry the painting in appreciation for his help. He also sent the photographer large photographs of Booth and Barrett which became famous in art circles. Courtesy of the Douglas County Historical Museum.

CHILDREN'S PICTURES A SPECIALTY. While in Bismarck, Barry advertised the instantaneous process due to his newest camera and large skylight in the studio. The "beauty of the baby" could be transferred to paper between the laughs and cries. Years later, he continued to take photographs of children as this unidentified photo shows. Courtesy of the Douglas County Historical Museum.

NORTH DAKOTA CONSTITUTIONAL CONVENTION 1880's. Photo by Barry. Courtesy of the Douglas County Historical Museum.

CHAPTER NINE
SUPERIOR 1890-1897

On May 15, 1890, the Superior Daily Call had this to say about a new resident. "Today there came among us the great Sioux Charmer, D. F. Barry of Bismarck, North Dakota. For lo these many years, he has with equal delight made photographs of Gall, John Grass, and all the other big Sioux and lawmakers of Dakota. As special artist for Frank Leslie's illustrated paper, he sketched the Custer Battlefield and Little Big Horn and all the characters who survived. Even "Old Sitting Bull" sat down in captivated meditation and looked his most human before Barry's camera. The Call hopes he will stay with us."

When the Barrys arrived in Superior, Wisconsin, it had a population of 28,635. Superior was subdivided into South Superior, East End, West Superior (West End), Superior City (Middletown), and Central Park.

The city had eight banks with $660,000 in capital. There were five railroads which terminated in Superior. They were: The Northern Pacific, Great Northern, Chicago, St. Paul, Minneapolis and Omaha, St. Paul and Duluth, and the South Shore and Atlantic. Sixty-four passenger trains and thirty freight trains arrived and departed daily.

Some of the major businesses and manufacturers included: American Steel Barge Co., West Superior Iron and Steel Co., Standard Iron Works, Warehouse and Builders Supply Co., Duff Forge Co., Lehigh Coal and Iron Co., Northwestern Adamant Plaster Co., Superior Cut Stone Co., Labelle Wagon Works Co., Webster Manufacturing Co., and three saw mills on Connor's point.

There was at this time much building going on in Superior. In 1890, 1883 buildings were built in the city, many of which were family dwellings. It was during this time of rapid growth that the Superior Trade and Commerce Building, the Watkins Block, New York Block and the West Superior, Tower, Broadway and Euclid Hotels were built. There were also 14 churches and 13 schools in Superior when the Barrys arrived.

In 1891 Barry established his studio-gallery at 522 Tower Avenue in West Superior. He and Patti lived in rooms at the back.

Superior was first settled as a town site in 1853. It was plotted in 1854 by three different townsite companies: "Superior", "Superior City," and "Middletown" (between the two).

The city of Superior was incorporated by a special act of the Wisconsin Legislature April, 1889. West Superior was plotted in 1885 on the apex of a plateau of 37 square miles on a diamond shaped peninsula surrounded on three sides by Lake Superior, St. Louis Bay and the St. Louis River.

In 1886 there was an influx of population to the city. The population in 1889 was 14,239 and grew in 1890. It was destined to become in the very near future a great commercial and manufacturing city. It was expected to draw from the cities and towns of the west and northwest especially men of wealth, talent and energy who usually flock to a metropolis, thus making it one of the most fascinating of cities.

522 TOWER AVENUE. In the space between the two buildings, Barry first settled in Superior. Barry established his studio-gallery in West Superior. He and Mrs. Barry lived in rooms at the back. Photo by Bob Heski.

BACK OF BARRY'S CATALOGUE. Courtesy of the Denver Public Library, Western History Dept.

CELEBRATION AND BARBECUE on arrival of first street car in South Superior, Sep. 14, 1892. Courtesy of the Douglas County Historical Museum.

BEMIS BAG AND PAPER COMPANY before 1908. Photo by Barry. Courtesy of the Douglas County Historical Museum.

CELEBRATION AND BARBECUE in observance of the arrival of the first street cars in South Superior. Sep. 14, 1892. Courtesy of the Douglas County Historical Museum.

D. F. BARRY'S
CATALOGUE OF

NOTED INDIAN CHIEFS.

522 TOWER AVENUE,
WEST SUPERIOR, - WISCONSIN.

FRONT OF BARRY'S CATALOGUE. Barry had a catalogue made up which listed most of his photographs. He would send them out upon request. Courtesy of the Denver Public Library, Western History Dept.

Superior was described as an inchoate city, or a city in progress of creation, and any description given of it must necessarily be incomplete.

The city had 3 daily newspapers in 1891: The Evening Telegram, Superior Daily and Weekly Call, and the Daily Leader. It also had many papers that came out once a week. These included the Superior Critic, Superior Times, South Superior Sun, The Superior Posten-Hotel Tower Block, The Superior Wave, and the Superior Zieutung.

Barry made friends easily with the people of Superior. He sent the editor-in-chief of "The Superior Leader" framed portraits of half a dozen celebrated Indian chiefs with his compliments.

A newspaper article had this to say of Barry. "He is posted in the inner and unwritten history of the later Indian wars, and the cause which led to them. He is a fluent talker and can supplement the historical incidents of which his photographs are reminders with recitals of events which have never appeared in print. A visit to his parlors will repay anyone for the time spent in looking over his collection of Indian photographs and rare historical relics."

In 1892 Superior was the "eye of the northwest." It was also dubbed the home of the whaleback. Captain Alexander McDougall invented the whaleback, a pig-nosed boat so constructed that the hatches could be closed down so the waves would wash over the craft and do no harm. Right after the city was incorporated, a movement was made to build the whalebacks in Superior. By 1892 there were thirty-one built to date at the Superior shipyards.

McDougall was directly responsible for the great boom in the city of Superior during the years 1890-1892. The American Steel Barge Co. was organized by A. D. Thompson of Duluth, Colgate Hoyt and Associates of New York and Capt. McDougall.

In all, forty-five freight whalebacks and one passenger ship were turned out in Superior, and subsidiary concerns were started on the Atlantic and Pacific coasts.

At the time of the American Steel Barge Company's start in Superior, the West Superior Iron and Steel Com-

CAPTAIN ALEXANDER McDOUGAL'S BOYS. Photo by Barry. Courtesy of the Douglas County Historical Museum.

4TH OF JULY PARADE in 1892 at Superior, Wisconsin. Courtesy of the Douglas County Historical Museum.

FIRST HIGH SCHOOL in West Superior, Wisconsin. Courtesy of the Douglas County Historical Museum.

THE WATKINS BLOCK, West Superior. The Barrys lived at 43 Watkins block from 1892-1897. Courtesy of the Douglas County Historical Museum.

108

READY FOR ACTION while in New York, Barry methodically traveled to Saratoga Springs to watch the races. Photo by Barry. Courtesy of the Douglas County Historical Museum.

CHIEF JOSEPH AND CAPTAIN JEROME with Buffalo Bill's horses. Photo by Barry. Taken at Madison Square Garden. In the author's collection.

ONE OF BARRY'S THEATRE FRIENDS. While in New York, the Barrys met many actors and actresses. Courtesy of the Douglas County Historical Museum.

CHAPTER ELEVEN
BACK TO SUPERIOR 1898-1925

The Duluth News Tribune ran an article in the fall of 1898: "David F. Barry of New York, better known as "the frontier photographer," was in Duluth last evening calling on friends. Mr. Barry is known in the office of every publication of note in the country on account of his Indian pictures. He said, 'I did well in New York, but somehow I had a longing to return to the west from the first day I landed there. A man who has lived in the west for as many years as I have cannot go east and be thoroughly contented. I have many friends in West Superior and Duluth and they are urging me to return here.

"I have had several places under consideration, but I think I shall locate in West Superior. Times have improved at the head of the lakes very much since I went away.'

"Mr. Barry is accompanied by Mrs. Barry. They came up the lakes and are visiting head of the lake friends. "Jack" the Scotch terrier that followed Mr. Barry during many years of his life on the frontier and who barked at Sitting Bull, Rain-in-the-Face, Gall and other noted chiefs, is here also."

The Barrys returned to Superior and took up residence at 1312 Tower Avenue. They lived in rooms in the back of the studio. As time went by, they renewed friendships and established themselves once again in the town.

1900 was a year of city building in Superior. There was also an increase in growth and prosperity especially in rural districts. The year of 1905 showed the largest increase in population in 12 years — 2,205.

Rain-in-the-Face's niece wrote Barry a letter from Rain's death bed in 1905.
"Mr. D. F. Barry:

I will let you know of the death of your old friend, Rain-in-the-Face. His death occurred on the twelfth of August 9 - 10 o'clock in the evening. Just before he died he asked me to do this and also he sends his regards to you and a last shake of your hand. Thanks for all you have done for him while you were here. And if possible, after death, he will think of you and pray for you.

I am a niece of Rain-in-the-Face and I desire to have a picture of you and him together. Will close with my best regards and wishes.
Very respectfully,

                                                                                    Rosie B. Soldur"

The population in 1907 was 41,760. "Nothing in life stands still; everything improves or deteriorates." Superior didn't grow for a number of years and it must have been very discouraging to those loyal citizens, so firm in their belief of the city. Superior increased to 42,595 in 1908. During this year Barry tried out one of those new fangled telephones and had the number: Bell phone 4006-K.

D. F. Barry received a letter from Buffalo Bill stating that the Big Exhibition would be in Superior on Twenty-Ninth Street and Tower Avenue. The original site on Belknap Street was at first scheduled to accommodate the Wild West Show, but owing to heavy rains the land was immersed in water. Thus the new site was selected.

There would be two exhibitions, rain or shine. The matinee in the afternoon exhibited all the features to be seen at night.

In the letter Buffalo Bill stated that the final appearance would be in Superior.

The combination of Buffalo Bill's Wild West Show and Pawnee Bill's Far East lent a variety to the many exciting acts.

Buffalo Bill was personally met at the Union Station by D. F. Barry. The two old friends rode down Tower Avenue under the watchful scrutiny of the pedestrians who craned for a farewell look at the pioneer of the plains.

They enjoyed a little chat, reminiscent and solicitous in Barry's studio. It was the last appearance of the old scout in Superior and the two made the most of their brief meeting. The show then moved to Superior on 32nd Avenue West.

Barry went to Duluth to visit the Wild West Show. He wrote Burke, representative of Col. W. F. Cody, Buffalo Bill's Wild West Show which was reinforced by Pawnee Bill's Far East. "I hate to call you wrong, I always thought that though you were a stickler for conservative statements, you always reached the truth. To this exhibition this year you have not done justice, why, it is far beyond your claims and excels anything in the exhibition line ever given."

William D. Coxey, the veteran "man ahead" for the Barnum and Bailey Shows, in the little magazine "Coxey's," a periodical of comment, complimented Barry in his magazine writing: "If chance, business, or pleasure ever take you to Superior, Wisconsin, drop in and get acquainted with D. F. Barry.

"Mr. Barry is a photographer, but not an ordinary photographer. He has never been content to "take" ordi-

TWO FRIENDS OF THE WEST. D. F. Barry and Major James McLaughlin former Indian agent for Standing Rock Agency. Taken at Barry's studio in 1915 when McLaughlin was in Superior with a commission to divide lands of the LaPoint band of Chippewa Indians. Photo by Barry. Courtesy of the Denver Public Library, Western History Dept.

nary pictures. Among his extraordinary pictures are original photographs of some of the most famous Indian chiefs that have lived in recent years."

As sections of the city of Superior grew, many of the old buildings were torn down as new ones were built. In 1913, Barry packed up his gallery and moved from 1312 Tower next door to a new building at 1316 Tower Avenue. The population of Superior was then 45,000. The Barrys lived in rooms in the rear of the studio.

Occasionally, Barry wrote articles in various newspapers and magazines related to some phase of the Custer Battle. He wrote one for the Bismarck Daily Tribune which commented on it in an editorial. It attracted widespread attention. He received complimentary clippings from a number of papers in which his article was referred to as authentic on a number of disputed details. The article was written in observance of the 37th Anniversary of the Custer Battle.

He also wrote an article on the battle which was published in the Superior Telegram, and was profusely illustrated with his photographs.

Barry didn't advertise in the newspapers much. He relied on his name and reputation. He had an awning with his name and trade upon it which decorated the studio front. On the back of his photographs he also labeled his name and address.

The Manchester, England, Geographical Society, world-wide in its researches and in the distribution of its reports, issued a pamphlet upon the subject, Prehistoric Man at the Headwaters of the Mississippi. "The author is honorable J. V. Brower of St. Paul," the pamphlet stated.

"Mr. Brower has placed great reliance in D. F. Barry, the photographer of West Superior, for illustrations and information concerning the Indian tribes of the west.

"Many of the illustrations in the English publication by the Manchester Society were by Mr. Barry and one of them is one of Mr. Barry and his friend Rain-in-the-Face."

The Superior City Directory of 1914 read: Barry, D. F., photographer of historic Indian chiefs, 1316 Tower Avenue, phone Broad 6-K rooms the same.

HANDSOME MRS. BARRY. Photo by Barry. Courtesy of the Denver Public Library, Western History Dept.

Major McLaughlin, inspector for the Dept. of the Interior, and Dr. W. M. Wooster, and L. M. McPherson of the Indian Office were in Superior to determine who was entitled to share in the division of the funds and lands owned by the La Point band of Chippewa Indians.

He visited Barry. Members of the commission were in Superior for hearings in the Hotel Superior. They returned to Ashland, Wisconsin, which was the headquarters for the investigation.

Barry took a photograph of Chief Blackbird, 79-year-old chief of the La Point band of Chippewa Indians, and added it to his extensive collection of photographs and relics.

Barry corresponded frequently with Elizabeth Custer, widow of the general. At this time, Mrs. Custer was living in New York City.

Barry sent her innumerable photographs for use in her articles and the books she wrote. She always spoke highly of Barry whenever his name was mentioned. Barry often stated that Mrs. Custer and he were "close and tighter than the bark of an old hickory nut tree," and

"Mrs. Custer is a personal friend of mine."

In commenting on an article written by E. S. Curtis, Barry said, "She will be hurt by the article and I am surprised that the alleged historian should have been taken in by the lying Crows.

"It is easy to condemn after the event, but he is a fool who would sit in judgment on a man acting under the conditions that confronted General Custer. He may have been wrong in his judgment, but he was a brave man and a capable general.

"Rain-in-the-Face was a true and loyal friend of mine and was not as cruel as some think. He was of a kindly disposition and ever after spoke of Mrs. Custer. Whenever I wrote to her I would mention this and she seemed very pleased."

Whenever the anniversary of the Custer Battle came about, Barry would write an article on the battle. Barry was emphatic in many instances in his criticism of the circulation of reports from Indians who had no new authentic information on the subject.

He had only contempt for "those modern parlor car

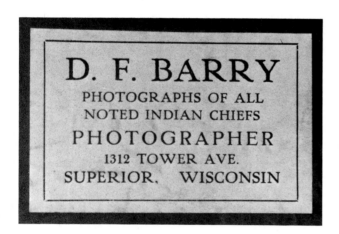

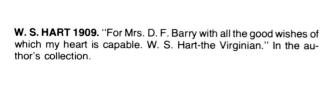

W. S. HART 1909. "For Mrs. D. F. Barry with all the good wishes of which my heart is capable. W. S. Hart-the Virginian." In the author's collection.

120

BUFFALO BILL CODY. Barry said, "I've never had a better or truer friend". Photo by Barry. Courtesy of the Douglas County Historical Museum.

WHILE BARRY WAS IN NEW YORK, he asked his friend Buffalo Bill if he would include Superior in his Wild West Show itinerary. In mid July of 1926, the Sells Floto Circus and Buffalo Bill Wild West Show visited Superior. This photograph was taken by Barry at the last performance. Courtesy of the Douglas County Historical Museum.

historians'' who wrote articles or books with new details of the fight.

On the 39th Anniversary of the battle, Barry wrote, ''There is one lady in America to whom this will be a sad day. She is Mrs. George A. Custer, widow of the great general. She will undoubtedly recall today the two brave generals who took part. The first was General Custer who fell in the battle, and the other Chief Gall.''

Barry wrote ''a memory of the Custer fight,'' which appeared in the Sports Afield magazine. He related many little known facts about the battle which set right a number of erroneous beliefs. Among the things he brought out were that Commanche, the horse which became famous because it was the only animal found alive on the field, was not ridden by General Custer as was generally believed, but by Captain Myles W. Keogh.

Also during 1915, Barry wrote an article on Sitting Bull, the famous Sioux warrior whom he referred to as the ''most thoroughly advertised Indian of the old frontier.'' The article appeared in the October issue of ''The American Patriot.'' Both articles were illustrated with photographs taken by Barry.

1916 was the 40th Anniversary of the Custer Battle. It was a time of reflection and tribute by many as the year came and went. Many books and articles were written about the Custer Battle. Many people wrote Barry for photographs and information. Movie star Bill Hart talked at length to Gertrude Gordon, a writer for Motion Picture Magazine, about Indians and the development of the northwest. The article was in the November issue.

After telling much of the Custer fight and the events leading up to it, Mr. Hart said, ''a great deal of my information was given to me by D. F. Barry of Superior, Wisconsin. Barry, I firmly believe, knows more of the real history of the frontier days than does any other man living or dead. He speaks the Sioux language fluently, and is one of the squarest men that ever lived and compared to his array of knowledge of the west, which he has at his fingers' ends, mine is that of an infant.''

Barry said, ''Except for the Christmas rush of my photography business in Superior, I might have been at the battle of Wounded Knee and in that vicinity at the

CUSTER'S LAST RALLY painted by John Mulvaney. Barry sent him photographs and information to work from. Courtesy of the Custer Battlefield Museum.

time Sitting Bull was killed."

Barry gave many photographs to Hart. Mr. Hart also purchased a number of photographs between 1920 and 1928. There are more than one hundred and fifty Barry photographs in the W. S. Hart County Museum collection as well as several letters between the two men.

As war fever broke out in Europe, and America subsequently entered the First World War, Superior did her share of war work. People flocked there from all parts of the country to work in the shipyards, and to make munitions for the war effort. The population of Superior increased.

Another boat for Uncle Sam was launched through the ice. The "War Otter" was a Frederikstadt type of boat. It was taken over by the U.S. Emergency Fleet Corporation. It was a sister ship to the "War Signal" and "War Chant" two Frederikstadts built at the Superior yards.

The ice was so thick in the slip that it was necessary to use dynamite to break it up, and seven to ten feet in thickness was taken out of the pocket. An entire night and days' work by a large crew of men was necessary to clear the slip of the ice blockade.

The men of the yards kept on with their work during the launching, which in former days meant a holiday for them.

The population of Superior in 1920 was 62,918. Photographs taken by Barry were used to illustrate a 431 page history of North Dakota, "Out Where the West Begins," by Zena Irma Trinka.

Dexter Fellows, representing the Ringling Bros. and Barnum Circus paid a social call on Barry. Barry made his acquaintance in the west and east as a result of his unique experiences and unduplicated collection of photographic plates acquired in the Dakotas. The circus played at the West End grounds on Thursday, August 25, 1921.

In 1922, Lewis F. Crawford of Bismarck wrote a letter to Barry concerning his old plates and his Indian collection. Barry replied, "I regret to inform you that I didn't keep all my old plates. I destroyed them. I kept only plates that interested me. I have willed all my large

LAUNCHING OF THE JAMES H. HOYT June 17, 1902. Courtesy of the Douglas County Historical Museum.

BARRY AND "JACK, HIS HORSE". A self portrait taken between 1897-1898. Courtesy of the Denver Public Library, Western History Dept.

124

GENERAL MILES. The General who was making history when the West was frontier. He rose from the ranks, was considerate and kind to his men and enjoyed the confidence and esteem of all with whom he came in contact. It was General Miles who exposed the rotten corned beef that authorities were issuing to the soldiers. The administration gave him the worst of it for telling the truth. Photo by Barry. In the author's collection.

MOURNERS AT MAJOR JAMES McLAUGHLIN'S FUNERAL
(left to right) D. F. Barry; A. G. Wells; Red Tomahawk; Capt.
I. P. Baker. Photo by Barry. Courtesy of the Smithsonian Institution, National Anthropological Archives, Bureau of American Ethnology.

THE SUMMER CAPITAL. Webster Memorial Bldg. used as President Coolidge's office during the summer of 1928 when he spent his vacation on the Brule River. Courtesy of the Douglas County Historical Museum.

CHAPTER TWELVE
WANING YEARS 1925-1934

As the year of 1925 came to a close, a renewed interest in the Custer fight became apparent. Mrs. Custer asked Barry if he would be on the National Custer Committee for the Fiftieth Anniversary of the Battle in 1926.

Others on the National Committee included Mrs. George A. Custer; Mrs. Mary Roberts, noted novelist; General Charles King; Ralph Budd, President of the Great Northern Railway; as well as other national figures, including senators and governors of Montana and Wyoming.

General E. S. Godfrey, a survivor of the battle, personally asked Barry to attend the festivities. Barry left for the 50th Anniversary of the battle at 2:15 June 20th.

They traveled to the West by train. Barry said: "When we were on the way to the Custer Battlefield in June 1925, those people (people of Mandan, N.D.) arranged to have the Northern Pacific Railroad hold the Coast Limited for 30 minutes. They entertained Generals Godfrey and Hunter, and wives in our party, at the depot. We stopped ten minutes in Bismarck."

Barry was a bit pessimistic about going to the 50th Anniversary observance. On May 3, 1926, he wrote the following to General Godfrey: "The enclosed pamphlet rather astonishes me. To think those people are making this Fiftieth Anniversary a real state advertising medium. They started out saying the celebration was to be at Billings. They sent me a bundle of this stuff. You may not look at this in the same light that it appears to me. Forty years ago at the Tenth Anniversary, we didn't make use of that event to advertise any person or state. This doesn't look like the proper thing to do. Perhaps I am old style."

Barry was in for a bigger shock when he reached the Battlefield. "Three flying machines were soaring over that historic field."

The entourage moved from the Battlefield to Billings where they detrained and stayed at the Northern Hotel. Barry had a pleasurable visit with his friend Bill Hart.

Barry said, "Bill Hart is probably better acquainted with the west, which is usually a part of his picture, than any other actor."

Meanwhile, thousands gathered at the ruins of Custer's home at old Fort Lincoln near Mandan on the 50th Anniversary of the battle. Messages from President Coolidge, Secretary of War Dwight Davis, Secretary of the Interior Hubert Work, and other prominent personages were read at the services.

Among the speakers who paid tribute to Custer's band were Major General Benjamin Pore of Omaha, Nebraska, Commander of the Seventh Corps Area; John F. Stevens, who discovered Marias Pass and assisted in building the Panama Canal; Mr. Hannaford, Chairman of the Board of Directors of the Northern Pacific Railroad; and Dr. John Lee Coulter, President of the North Dakota Agriculture College.

General Godfrey came from his home in Cookstown, New Jersey, for the semi-centennial observances of the battle. Mrs. Godfrey, the Godfrey's son, and C. Creighton of Mandan, North Dakota, one of the troopers of the Old Seventh also attended.

A strange assorted crowd milled through the narrow street of Crow Agency adjacent to the battlefield. Indians rubbed shoulders with whites and troopers of the Old Seventh greeted men of the new.

Veterans of the Indian wars officially welcomed their national commander, Colonel John H. Brandt of Los Angeles, California. Colonel Fitshugh Lee, Commander of the Seventh Cavalry also attended. Four old veterans attended: W. C. Stewart of Helena, Montana; W. G. Slaper and A. C. Rallya of Los Angeles, California, and John C. Lockwood. Sioux, Crow and Cheyenne warriors who participated attended three-score strong.

A collection was taken at the observance to pay for the stone erected for the unknown soldier whose body was found some distance from the field.

The Montana Gazette called Barry a war photog-rapher. He furnished pictures to the National Custer Memorial Association for the nationwide publicity campaign to stimulate interest in the epochal Indian battle of the northwest, for the 50th Anniversary of the Custer Battle.

After the battle, Barry wanted a statue of Custer in Bismarck on the capital grounds. It could be erected by popular subscription. He wrote Mrs. Custer and other prominent people many times about the matter, but nothing was ever done about it.

Barry said the memory of Custer should be commemorated in marble and a monument erected to perpetuate his service.

Barry's nephew, Vernon Barry, visited Superior in 1926. He stayed at the Nichols Hotel. Vernon attended Western Military Academy in Alton, Illinois, and was dubbed "Captain" by his uncle.

In mid-July of 1926, the Sells Floto Circus and Buffalo Bill Wild West Show visited Superior. They set up at the old fair grounds, which is now part of the University of Wisconsin, Superior's "Fighting Yellow Jackets"

BARRY'S PHOTOGRAPHIC STUDIO, 1312 Tower Avenue. The photographs adorning the walls were taken by Barry. The folding camp chair in the foreground belonged to General Custer. Photo by Barry. Courtesy of the Denver Public Library, Western History Dept.

football field.

As the parade came through Superior, it traveled down Belknap Avenue and turned on to Tower Avenue. Barry watched the proceedings from his second story gallery at 1316 Tower Avenue. Tower Avenue was where Barry had paraded years before in the same carriage with Buffalo Bill Cody, in what he said was "one of the proudest moments of my life."

As some Indians in the parade rode by, one of them gave the sign of recognition and said he would come back.

As he sat in his studio on Sunday, July 18, 1926, Barry's door bell rang, and almost before he could reach the door, four stalwart Indians marched in. Barry immediately recognized the oldest of the quartet as the same boy who 39 years earlier he had photographed with his father, Sitting Bull. For more than 3 hours, these four Indians conversed with Barry in sign language and stared at the photographs and relics on the studio walls.

Barry took a few photographs of John and his friends in the studio and added them to his collection.

Barry and Nellie, a faithful old horse of the American Express Company, were friends. Barry learned to love horses and made friends with them wherever he went. Nellie, in her travels up and down Tower Avenue and around the city, used to stop in front of Barry's studio while the driver Walter Carlson made his deliveries. Knowing a horse's fondness for carrots, Barry used to carry a pocketful at times, and made friends with the animals by giving them the delectable vegetables. Nellie would rarely pass Barry's studio without looking up at the window with an expectant eye for carrots. Many times in the course of a day, Barry would meet the horse in the midst of a brisk gallop; she would draw up to the curb and sniff Mr. Barry's pockets for carrots. The horse at times would step onto the sidewalk in an attempt to follow Barry to the entrance leading to the studio.

The Buffalo Bill Museum asked Barry if he would send some of his photographs to the Buffalo Bill Museum in Cody, Wyoming. They had a room that they were putting in. He personally wrote many influential people asking them to donate photographs to the room.

SELLS FLOTO CIRCUS ADVERTISEMENT. Photo by Bob Heski. Courtesy of the Buffalo Bill Museum.

Doc W. F. Carver, greatest rifle shot of the old west, sent Barry a letter which said in part, "Long years have passed since we met, yes, it is at least 40 years since I saw you in Bismarck. I followed the old trail until it was all broken up by the Indians' great friend, the white man. I am not quite sure, but I think I have been dead for the last 20 or 30 years. As you know, in my heart, I am a real Indian. Some day soon the wind will blow me over the divide and then they will plant me in the tree tops where I will dry up. If I miss you here on earth, Barry, I hope to meet you in the happy hunting grounds."

Carver, the rifle shot, also known as "the evil spirit of the plains" was champion of the world in his time. He performed before presidents Grant and Hayes, the crowned heads of Europe and the governors of Australia. He shot in exhibition before the English Army at Aldershot, the German Army at Berlin, the Russian Cossacks at Warsaw, and the Russian Army at Moscow. His performances were startling, inasmuch as he shot at flying objects (and hit them) using a rifle with single bullets and not shot.

The Mandan North Dakota Daily Pioneer urged Barry to write about Indian history, especially how his photographs were taken. He never did.

In 1929, the Barrys rented from Mr. George G. Newton, who was in real estate. Mr. Newton had Barry take photographs of various homes and buildings for him in exchange for rent.

Superior in 1928-1929 was dubbed the summer capital of America. President Calvin Coolidge chose Cedar Island Lodge on the Brule River in Wisconsin for his 1929 vacation. Central High School was the location of the executive offices and general headquarters of the government.

Western reminiscences were exchanged between Barry and N. Edward Beck, general press representative of Miller Bros. 101 Ranch Wild West Show, which was coming to Superior. Many Indians of the old days were with the show, including Chief White Elk, second cousin of Steps, who was a brother of Joseph the Nez Perce. More than 30 years before, Steps was lost in a vast snow storm, his horse frozen to death and he himself lost both

MRS. BARRY. Photo by her husband. Courtesy of Mr. and Mrs. Vernon Barry.

AN OLDER BARRY. Notice the movement in the photograph. Something he wouldn't have done in his younger days. Photo by Barry. Courtesy of the Denver Public Library, Western History Dept.

legs and his right arm. A group of Sioux hunters found him and nursed him back to health.

Col. Zack T. Miller, director of the 101 Ranch Show signified his intention of selecting, while in Superior, a Barry picture to be hung with the Miller Bros. compliments of the Cody Museum.

When Barry saw a frog story in the Miles City Star, he sent the following note: "In the month of June in 1881 or 1882 at Fort Assiniboine, Montana, during the night, it rained frogs; thousands of them. You couldn't walk without stepping on them. During the guard mount it was hard for the band and soldiers to keep on their feet after dinner. The prisoners were ordered out to take the dead frogs up as quite an odor was coming from them. By two o'clock in the afternoon, all the live ones had passed on to the river.

"Yesterday, I received a letter from Mrs. Custer. She was much pleased with your editorial on the monument. She said she was going to write to you. I sent her a paper."

Tragedy struck Barry August 20, 1932. His wife died at their residence following a long illness that had kept her confined for two years.

Services were held at the Church of the Redeemer in East Superior. Reverend Henry Spencer officiated. Mrs. Barry was interred in the family plot in Greenwood Cemetery. Pall bearers were chosen from among the many friends of Mr. and Mrs. Barry. They included: William K. Link, Charles H. Sunderland, Gordon H. Blackburn and A. W. Elmgreen of Superior, and Charles D. Skillings and Albert Dodd of Duluth.

Numerous telegrams of condolence were received by Mr. Barry from friends in many states. Among them were messages from Mr. and Mrs. Joseph Scanlon and family, Miles City, Montana; Leon Shaw, Editor of the Billings Gazette; and George D. Mann, Editor of the Bismarck Tribune. Mrs. Barry was a woman of fine character and gentle nature. Her illness prevented her from taking an active part in the life of the city. Her passing was deeply regretted by her many friends who knew her for so many years.

In a letter to Mr. Frank Hutchinson, October 31,

BARRY PHOTOS presented to the Buffalo Bill Museum by Barry; originally displayed in the Barry Room of the old museum, they now adorn the walls in the lower level of the Cody Museum. Photo by Bob Heski. Courtesy of the Buffalo Bill Museum.

JOHN SITTING BULL (right) and friend taken in 1926 in Barry's studio, where the two were touring with one of the Wild West Shows. Photo by Barry. Courtesy of the Douglas County Historical Museum.

1930, Barry said, "I burned my will. I had willed all my large framed pictures to the North Dakota Historical Society. They had copied a number of my pictures and were selling them unmounted at thirty cents a piece, when I was getting $1.50 mounted. When I put in over fifty years getting this collection, only for a state to rob me of my efforts"—for North Dakota a tragic blunder on someone's part, for Superior, a blessing.

Bad luck continued to plague Barry. He was seriously injured in Duluth when an automobile crashed into the rear end of a street car in which he was a passenger at the intersection of Ninth Avenue West and Michigan Street. The street car had stopped to allow Mr. Barry to alight, when a large automobile crashed into the car from the rear. Mr. Barry, who was on the rear platform at the time, was knocked unconscious and sustained a deep gash over his forehead. He was given first aid treatment and was put under care of Dr. F. C. Sarazin.

In 1933, Barry sustained a bad fall and hurt his leg. It kept him primarily confined to his studio, except for his short walks to numerous hotels where he ate his meals.

Whenever he went out, he dressed in his best clothes and wore his wide-brimmed western hat. He cut a dashing figure even in older life with his large white mustache and complimentary remarks to whomever he met.

Mrs. George A. Custer died in New York City at the age of 91. Barry paid tribute to her, "I don't know what I can say that is fine enough for her. She was a remarkable woman."

Barry thought the city should rebuild the old stockade. "The citizens should take steps to acquire the site of the old stockade on the Superior bay front and arrange for the reproduction of the fortification built in the Civil War period to repel the attacks of Indians. They must build it soon for the men who helped to construct and defend the original stockade are passing fast and when they are gone there will be none who can direct its reproduction. It could be a meeting place for our Old Settlers Assoc."

Mr. John Kardon, a neighbor of Barry's, often would take him for automobile rides. One time while passing a cemetery, Barry said, "They'll be smoking cigars over

BARRY'S PHOTOGRAPHIC STUDIO, 1312 Tower Avenue. Many of the relics that adorned the walls were purchased by Barry or were given to him by the Indians he photographed. Photo by Barry. Courtesy of the Denver Public Library, Western History Dept.

PAWNEE BILL AND BUFFALO BILL. The two plainsmen turned showmen; each had his own show. They brought the west to the east. They combined their Wild West Shows and formed a partner-ship. Both were friends of photographer Barry. Photo by Barry. Courtesy of the Douglas County Historical Museum.

IN 1929, THE BARRYS were forced to move to 1312 Tower Avenue. They were getting old, and the photography business wasn't as profitable as it once had been. Barry was forced to do what he disliked the most—taking photographs of buildings to pay his rent. Barry advertised "photo's taken all styles". He advertised by his awning and by a wooden billboard outside the door leading to the studio. It can be seen behind the children in the photograph. Photo by Barry. Courtesy of the Douglas County Historical Museum.

our graves when we're gone, Johnny!''

Mr. Frank Hutchinson formerly of Bismarck, visited the museum of the American Indian in New York. He talked to Mr. George Heye about Barry and his valuable collection of photographs and Indian relics. Mr. Heye wanted Hutchinson to prevail upon Barry to make affidavits concerning each of his historical specimens. He also suggested that Hutchinson ask Barry to present his collection to his institution, or loan it for an indefinite period.

Barry was thinking of selling his collection to Hutchinson for fifteen hundred dollars, after refusing at one time to sell it for five thousand dollars. Hutchinson wanted an affidavit concerning the Rain-in-the-Face rifle that he purchased dirt cheap from Barry. Hutchinson wanted Barry to make affidavits regarding the many Indian relics and call in a notary public to acknowledge each one of the relics. He said that he would also pay for it. It was never done.

W. K. Link said of Barry, ''Yes, I knew he was broke and have known it for several years, and that is why I have been helping him. He was very proud and wouldn't talk about it, but I could tell from his actions just what his thoughts were and it is a great satisfaction to me to know that I was able to smooth out some of the rough spots for him and I took pleasure in doing so.

''I asked him why he didn't sell the relics, negatives, etc. and go to the hotel and live, but he wouldn't listen to that. On the contrary, he offered all these things to me at various times for nothing and I knew the motive prompted him to do so. He was generous to a fault.''

Barry couldn't bear the thought of parting with his collection, so he ignored the letters sent by Hutchinson.

On Feb. 5, 1934, Barry received a letter from Maryls Mae Kibbon saying: ''Some day your photos will be valued by our Sioux people as depicting part of their history. Right now it does not mean a great deal—the generations growing up will appreciate these.'' He previously had sent her some photos on request.

W. S. HART AND LUTHER STANDING BEAR. Photo by Barry, taken at the 50th Anniversary of the Custer Battle in 1926. Courtesy of the Douglas County Historical Museum.

THE LITTLE SHADOW CATCHER, photographer D. F. Barry in later years. After his wife's death, Barry took many of his meals at the Superior Hotel and other places where he would gather with a few chosen cronies and talk of days past. He was a familiar site in the port city of Superior as he walked the streets dressed in his best clothes alone with his memories. A self-portrait. Courtesy of the Denver Public Library, Western History Dept.

141

STATUE OF W. S. HART. Barry, Doc Carver, Pawnee Bill (Gordon W. Lilly) and Bill Hart were invited to Cody, Wyoming, for a dedication of the Buffalo Bill Museum. They were also invited to Billings, Montana, July 2-4 in 1927, for a celebration where a statue of Bill Hart and his horse was to be unveiled on July 4. Barry couldn't attend either celebration, but sent his regards. Given to Barry by Hart. Courtesy of the Douglas County Historical Museum.

D. F. BARRY

PHOTOGRAPHER

Tower Ave.   Superior, Wis.

CHIEF GALL.

OTOS OF NOTED INDIANS

Photos of Sitting Bull, Gall, Rain-in-Face, John Grass, Crow King, Long Dog, R
Cloud, American Horse, Curley Spotted Tail, Low Dog, Buffalo Bill, Chief Go

Chief Joseph, Good Horse, Bull Head, Custer Battle Field, General Custer, Benteen, Miles, Crook, G
frey, Major Reno, McDougall, Captain Tom Custer, Crow Foot, Sitting Bull's Family, Fort Linc

Charlie Reynolds, Horse Comanche, Crow Fly High, Thunder Hawk, Circling Bear, General George Forsy
Wild Horse, California Joe, Running Antelope, Fire Cloud, Red Horse, Young Man Afraid of Hors
Standing Holy, General Gibbon.

COLORFUL BARRY ENVELOPE. Barry didn't advertise in the newspapers much. He relied on his reputation. He did have these envelopes made as well as calling cards to achieve advertising results. Courtesy of Mr. and Mrs. Vernon Barry.

ELIZABETH B. CUSTER, widow of the general. She thought highly of Barry and asked him to be on the committee for the Fiftieth Anniversary of the Battle. She also bought many photos from him. In a letter to Mrs. Custer, Barry said, "There seems to be a lack of that spirit of loyalty and appreciation for the officers and men who fell fighting for the good of the country and the old frontier. I wanted to see the Fiftieth Anniversary a grand success. It simply passed my expectations. I put my heart and soul in that event. Many times during the day I thought of you. If you could only have been present for a few minutes to see the thousands who were there from ocean to ocean." Courtesy of the Denver Public Library, Western History Dept.

To that great Indianman
who I am proud to call
my friend L. A. Barry

Wm. S. Hart
Billings, Mont.

W. S. HART. Bill Hart gave a talk at the theatre in Billings after the Fiftieth Anniversary of the Custer fight. He paid General Custer a fine tribute. He also praised Barry's work that he had done for history in preserving pictures that cannot now be secured. The press of Billings and Miles City, Montana, also praised Barry and his work in articles. The papers adorned with his photographs went for one to two dollars each. Courtesy of the Douglas County Historical Museum.

BARRY AND SITTING BULL'S SON, JOHN SITTING BULL JR.
Photo taken in 1926 while John was in Superior with the combined Buffalo Bill Wild West Show and the Sells Floto Circus. A self photo. Courtesy of the Douglas County Historical Museum.

JOHN SITTING BULL. Taken in Superior in 1926 when John was touring the city with one of the Wild West Shows. Sitting Bull had three children by his first wife Seen By the Nation. They were Crow Foot, who died with his father; Standing Holy, a daughter; and John Sitting Bull. John was born a mute. He was deeply touched when shown photographs of his mother, father and sister. Barry found out that Standing Holy had died a few months before. John said, "He was alone in the world with no home to go to". Photo by Barry. Courtesy of the Smithsonian Institution, National Anthropological Archives, Bureau of American Ethnology Collection.

"CAPTAIN" VERNON BARRY. Barry's nephew Vernon visited his uncle in 1926. He attended the Western Military Academy in Alton, Illinois, therefore, he was given rank by his uncle. Photo by Barry. Courtesy of Mr. and Mrs. Vernon Barry.

CHAPTER THIRTEEN
END OF THE TRAIL

For a few years after his wife's death, Barry lived in semi-seclusion. His only wish was to live to be eighty years old.

He was always proud of the honor that he possessed. He was independent when it was necessary, but charitable to a fault, and always willing to bear his own cross without a murmur, and told his troubles to very few. As far as his domestic affairs were concerned, no one knew.

W. K. Link sent Barry's brother Mike a letter on March 3, 1934, it said, "Advising that brother Dave has been in bad shape for two or 3 weeks. Had doctor call and see him about 10 days ago. He has vomiting spells and does not seem to hold anything down in his stomach. It is my opinion he should be in the hospital where he could get proper medical attention, but he objects strenuously to leaving his present home."

Link had checked on Barry and found he was in considerable distress, and he asked a doctor to call and see him. The doctor immediately took him to the hospital and diagnosed the trouble as malignant stomach trouble—possibly cancer. Anyhow it caused stoppage of the bowels. He subsequently was carried unconscious to St. Mary's Hospital.

Barry had been failing for some time. About two years previously, he had some infection in his leg which had crippled him and it was impossible for him to get around.

If Barry had not been quite so old, with an invalid wife for years, and failing health himself in his last days, he might at this time have realized more fully the fruits of the efforts of his younger days.

Late reports from his bedside indicated that he was sinking gradually. John Kardon, local dry cleaner and a friend of Barry's, was visiting Barry when the sick man regained consciousness and said, "God bless you Johnny." With these few words David F. Barry left for the "long trail over the divide."

Barry died on Tuesday, March 6, 1934, at St. Mary's Hospital at 2 p.m. It was his eightieth birthday.

His funeral took place at the Superior Elk's Club. The remains of the Little Shadow Catcher were taken from the hospital to the LeSage Funeral Home. Later the remains were taken to the Elk's Club at noon to lie in state until the time of the services at 2:30 pm.

Rev. Harold Johns of the Episcopal Church of the Redeemer of East End officiated at the burial. The burial was at the family plot at Greenwood Cemetery, where Mrs. Barry was also buried.

Six Superior Eagle Boy Scouts, Jay Raaflaub, Donald Perry, Donald Ostlund, Robert Mathison, and Ellsworth and Warren Argetsinger were active pall bearers. John Dolan, another Boy Scout, blew taps on his bugle following the service.

Honorary pall bearers were the friends and associates of Barry. They included W. K. Link, G. H. Blackburn, Charles H. Sunderland, John Kardon, Dr. F. C. Sarazin, Clough Gates, and Gordon MacQuarrie

CHAPTER 14
HONORS BESTOWED

Throughout David F. Barry's long and colorful life, many honors were bestowed on him. He had many friends and associates who cherished his friendship as he cherished theirs.

One of his most cherished friends was Colonel W. F. Cody. Speaking of Col. Cody, the pioneer photographer said, "I never had a better friend in my life. He was a striking man—the sort of a fellow who made you turn around and look at him as you passed by. I had frequent visits with him at the Coliseum Theatre in Chicago when he was there with a show. When I had my art show and gallery in New York, I also contacted Buffalo Bill many times when he was playing at Madison Square Garden."

On June 19, 1933, Barry wrote J. D. Scanlon of Miles City, Montana, saying, "Some years ago Buffalo Bill invited Pawnee Bill and myself to come to Cody in the fall and visit with him, as he wanted to show us where he hoped to be buried—on the hill at Cody. He said from this spot there would be a good view of the Shoshone Valley. His wish at that time was to be buried at Cody. I believe that if you were talking to Pawnee Bill, he would recall the occasion."

There were many such incidents in the lives of Dave Barry and Colonel Cody which serve to illustrate that there were warm contacts between them.

On July 4, 1933, Barry received his most single honor when a bronze tablet was unveiled at Cody, Wyoming, where many of his pictures are displayed in the Barry Room of the Cody Museum. The inscription of the tablet reads "To David F. Barry, famous pioneer photographer of noted Indians, friend of and ardent admirer of W. F. (Buffalo Bill) Cody, this room of historic and artistic pictures is respectfully dedicated."

Because of his failing health, Barry was unable to attend the dedication at which his friend J. D. Scanlan made the chief address.

The tablet took the form of an engraved history of the life and work of Mr. Barry. It was placed on the western door of the Barry Room.

The ceremony of unveiling the Barry Room tablet was in the hands of a small group of famous western figures, with members of the Cody family. The various friends and admirers of Barry who contributed pictures to the Barry Room were guests of honor at the program. There was a distinct historical and western atmosphere.

On June 15, 1933, Barry wrote a letter to Joe Scanlan to accept this honor:
"Dear Joe:

I am in no shape to go to Cody, much as I would like. Please don't say much about me. I put over 50 years hard work getting the collection—nothing like it in the country. I am proud of the Barry Room in the

Cody Museum. More particularly because of my love for my dear old friend Buffalo Bill. The public is not interested in me. The less said, the better. I would love to see the room, but—

Sincerely yours,
Dave"

On July 4, 1933, Scanlan made the following remarks at the dedication of the Barry Room in the Cody Museum at Cody, Wyoming.

"It is an inspiration to me to be in this magnificent museum building today, which perpetuates the memory of Colonel Wm. F. Cody, whose adventurous, daring and romantic exploits have made him one of the immortals of the West. Personally I desire to express my appreciation for the honor which the Cody family has conferred upon me by inviting me to participate in the ceremonies incident to the formal dedication of the Barry Room.

"Yes, Buffalo Bill loved the West, and that is why the West loves Buffalo Bill, and no book on our library shelves is more popular in the West than "Buffalo Bill's Own Story". I am not here, however, to eulogize Colonel Wm. F. Cody. I would consider it a presumption on my part, were I to attempt to do so. His fame will carry on down through the annals of time, and generations will continue to pay homage to him after you and I will have reached the end of that long trail. I have, however, been delegated to represent on this memorable occasion a distinguished gentleman, who, while not having scaled the highest pinnacles of fame in the romance of the West, has nevertheless played a most prominent part in preserving the pictoral traditions of the hectic days of conflict between the Indians and the whites. He is the gentleman in whose honor the Cody family unveils the bronze memorial tablet today—my true and beloved friend, David F. Barry of Superior. Having known David F. Barry intimately from my boyhood days, I am naturally deeply impressed with the significance of this occasion. In the language of the west, they "don't make 'em any better". He is whole-souled, generous and kind, a square shooter, liked, trusted, and respected by his fellow men and he, in turn, loves his friends. What greater tribute can I pay him? He is in the twilight of life. Just a few months ago, he lost his wife to whom he was greatly attached. Following this he suffered an injury to his leg, which keeps him constantly under doctor's care, and from which we trust he will soon recover. Otherwise, he would be here today in person, to accept this bronze tablet unveiled in his honor and likewise to express his sincere appreciation

TENTATIVE TIMING SCHEDULE

S. S. "DAVID F. BARRY"

AUGUST 21ST, 1943

HULL   239TH SHIP

1:02	Ten minute warning whistle
1:03	Master of Ceremonies, Mr. Todd Woodell, will introduce the Singing Sentinels who will sing the Star Spangled Banner.
1:04½	Master of Ceremonies will introduce Mr. James P. O'Leary.
1:07	Master of Ceremonies will introduce - Master Michael O'Leary who will present flowers to Mrs. James P. O'Leary and Miss JoAnn Hoffman
1:08½	Master of Ceremonies will introduce Father A. J. Gelinas of St. Mary's Cathedral who will give the invocation.
1:09	Invocation
1:10½	Master of Ceremonies will turn the microphone over to Del von Zethen who will describe the burning of the plates.
1:12	Ship is launched.

- - - - - - - - - - - - -

LAUNCHING OF THE S. S. DAVID F. BARRY August 21, 1943, by the Oregon Shipbuilding Corporation, Portland, Oregon. Courtesy of Mr. and Mrs. Vernon Barry.

to the Cody family for the thoughtful and generous spirit which prompted the remembrance. In his absence, I will act for him, although I can assure you that if he were present himself, the formality of acceptance would be more gracious, although less ostentatious. But, from the distance, Dave Barry, at this moment gives deep and heartfelt expression of his gratitude."

The Columbus, Wisconsin Republican had this to say:

"Our older residents will remember D. F. Barry, a former resident of Columbus. Mr. Barry has a national reputation as a famous pioneer photographer of Indians of the old west". The Duluth Herald in a recent issue devoted three columns to Mr. Barry when a bronze tablet was erected at Cody, Wyoming, in his honor at the Buffalo Bill Museum.

The Barry Room consisted largely of Indian photos taken by Barry and existed for a few years until additional Buffalo Bill items were acquired which eventually filled the entire space.

The old museum was abandoned in 1967 because of possible fire damage and the museum moved to a new two million dollar building which was dedicated in 1969. Many of the Barry photos are still on exhibit in various sections of the museum.

In the field of frontier photography David F. Barry certainly deserves considerable recognition. His invaluable contributions to history are represented in many museums and historical societies around the United States.

Many of the Barry photographs in the W. S. Hart County Museum collection were gifts from the photographer to Mr. Hart.

Mr. Hart also wrote many books. One book from a series of three called "Injun and Whitey" contained information on David F. Barry. The books were written primarily for boys and interested adults.

In the twentieth chapter of the book "Injun and Whitey to the Rescue" Hart told of Custer's last stand, in which Mr. Barry was mentioned.

During World War II many liberty ships were built to help the wartime effort. The name David F. Barry was

IDENTIFICATION OF VESSEL

NAME(S) OF VESSEL	DATES OF OPERATION UNDER EACH NAME
David F. Barry	1943-1946

TONNAGE	RIG	DATE BUILT	PLACE BUILT
gross 7176.49 6653.68 net	Steam Screw	1943	Portland, Oregon

HOME PORT(S)	OPERATOR(S)
Master, Aug. 14, 1943 Edward A. Mortensen	
Master, Aug. 28, 1943 A. A. Kretchmar	Still master 23 July, 1946

ADDITIONAL INFORMATION OR REMARKS

Official Number 244,130

assigned by the U.S. Maritime Commission in Washington, D.C. to the Oregon Shipbuilding Corporation. Liberty ships were named for distinguished Americans in many fields. Barry's name was submitted by the North Dakota Historical Society.

The S. S. David F. Barry was launched on August 21, 1943, at 1:12 p.m. by the Oregon Shipbuilding Corporation in Portland, Oregon.

The S. S. David F. Barry plied the waters off Puget Sound and southeastern Alaska.

The naming of the ship was revealed in Superior through a letter to the city manager from the ship's captain A. A. Kretchmar, M.M., asking for information about Barry and for his picture. The letter was referred to Vivien G. Dube, curator at the Douglas County Museum. A picture of Barry was sent to Captain Kretchmar by Mrs. Dube and was hung in the ship's dining salon.

In 1959 the S.S. Barry was sold to the Polish Gov-

ernment and the name changed to Kopalnia Bobrek.

The Kopalnia Bobrek was operated in deep sea tramping, especially in the Mediterranean Sea range.

On December 27, 1971, the SS Kopalnia Bobrek was sold to the Spanish firm Revalorizacion de Materials S.A. BILBAO.

Today Barry's photographs may be viewed at the Denver Public Library; the W. S. Hart County Museum in Newhall, California; the North Dakota Historical Society; the Library of Congress, Washington, D.C. (Usher L. Burdick collection); Custer Battlefield National Monument; and the Douglas County Historical Society, Superior, Wisconsin; as well as in many individual collections.

Perhaps, as time goes by, the true worth of the Little Shadow Catcher's work will be fully realized. His remarkable photographs will give him rank with Remington and Russell in preserving in picture the stirring events in the winning of the west.

S/S KOPALNIA BOBREK, formerly the S.S. David F. Barry. It was sold to the Polish Government in 1959. Courtesy of the Polish Steamship Company.

					rf 6″	WB699t				
5193371	**KOPALNIA BOBREK**	7221		PR	1943	Oregon S.B. Corp.--Pld	S		T 3Cy. 622 940 & 1778×1219 mm	
SPNQ	exArta–59 exOakland–56	4429			441′ 6″ 57′ 0″ 27′ 7½″		5 Ho 60½′, 72½′, 49½′, 44½′, 69′	2500ihp		1032t (o.f)
	exDavid F. Barry–47	10457	Classed LR until 6/62		417′ 9″ 56′ 11″ 37′ 4″		G.562608 B.499573	Iron Fireman Mfg Co.		Pld
Df Esd	**Polish Government**				2 dks, 3rd dk fwd		5 Ha (35½′, 35½′, 19½′, 35½′, 35½′ × 19½′)	3×20kW 115V d.c.		11k
Rdr	Polish Steamship Co.				rf 3½″		10W Der 1(50) 1(15) 10(5)		
RTm/h	Szczecin	Polish							
5193383	**KOPALNIA CZELADZ**	7252		PR	1943	Bethlehem-Fairfield—Bal	S		T 3Cy. 622 940 & 1778×1219 mm	
SPQW	exLedbury–61 exAlpha Vaal–48	4263			441′ 8″ 57′ 0″ 27′ 9½″		5 Ho 60½′, 74½′, 50′, 39½′, 70′	2500ihp		1119t (o.f)

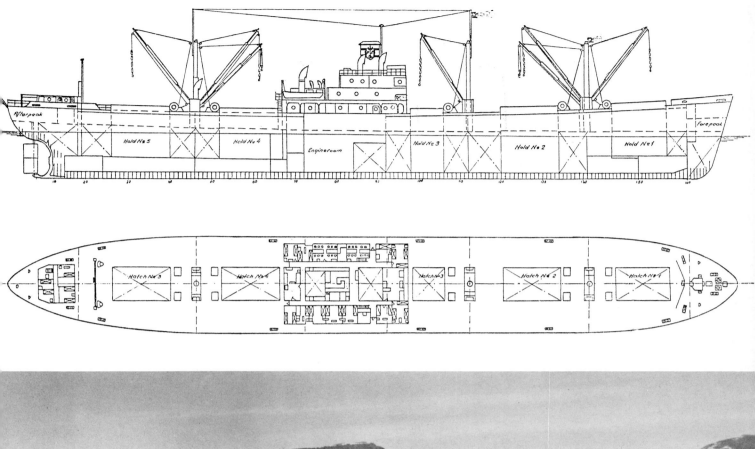

THE BUFFALO BILL HISTORICAL CENTER, Cody, Wyoming. The museum was moved into this two million dollar building which was dedicated in 1969. Many of the Barry photos originally hung in the Barry Room are on exhibit in various sections of the museum. Courtesy of Buffalo Bill Historical Center.

DISPLAYS IN THE BUFFALO BILL HISTORICAL CENTER,
Cody, Wyoming. Photo by Bob Heski. Courtesy of the Buffalo Bill
Historical Center.

DISPLAYS IN THE BUFFALO BILL HISTORICAL CENTER,
Cody, Wyoming. Photo by Bob Heski. Courtesy of the Buffalo Bill
Historical Center.

THE BUFFALO BILL MUSEUM in Cody, Wyoming, established in 1927, home of the Barry Room. Courtesy of the Buffalo Bill Historical Center, Cody, Wyoming.

THE PLAINS INDIAN MUSEUM located in the lower level of the Buffalo Bill Historical Center. Barry photographs adorn the walls. Photo by Bob Heski. Courtesy of the Buffalo Bill Historical Center.

159

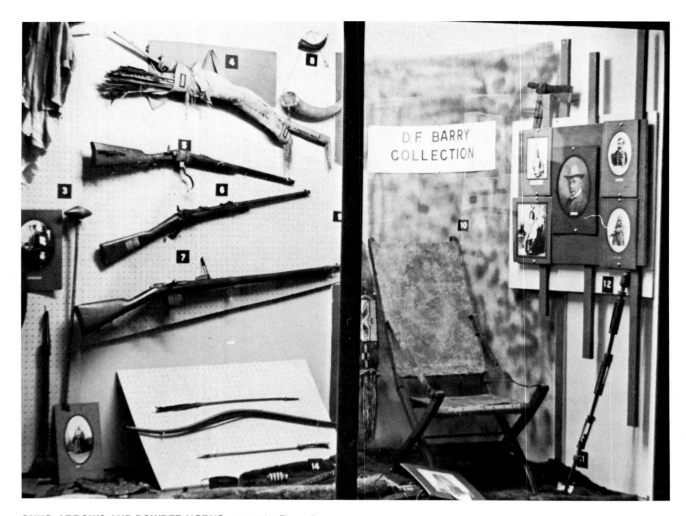

GUNS, ARROWS AND POWDER HORNS accent the Barry display. Some of the more interesting relics include: Long Feather's bow and arrows, Sitting Bull's 1859 Sharps carbine, a Custer fight carbine, and Custer's camp chair. Photo by Gary VanKauwenberg. Courtesy of the Douglas County Historical Museum.

MOCCASINS, top to bottom. Moccasin belonged to Crow Foot, Sitting Bull's son. Taken from his foot after he was killed; Chief Young-Man-Afraid-of-His-Horses' moccasins; and Chief John Grass's moccasins. Photo by Gary VanKauwenberg. Courtesy of the Douglas County Historical Museum.

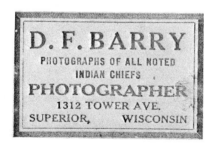

Judge Crazy Walking
Of the Indian Court at Standing Rock Agency

AT ONE TIME CRAZY Walking was a member of the Indian Police, who took part in the arrest of Sitting Bull, after the death of Chief Gall and John Grass. They were the judges of the Indian Court. Crazy Walking was appointed to the Judgeship of that Court which had been so ably filled by Chief Gall and John Grass. The late Chief Justice Waite of the United States Supreme Court visited at Standing Rock Agency years ago. When Gall and John Grass were told that Judge Waite was the Big Chief of that Court, at the Home of the Great Father, they said they would like to visit his Court and see how he runs things there.

In all the tribes of the North American Indians you will not find two Judges like Chief Gall and Chief John Grass. They were just and gave you all you were entitled to.

D. F. Barry
Photographer of Noted Indians
1512 Tower Avenue

Superior - - Wisconsin

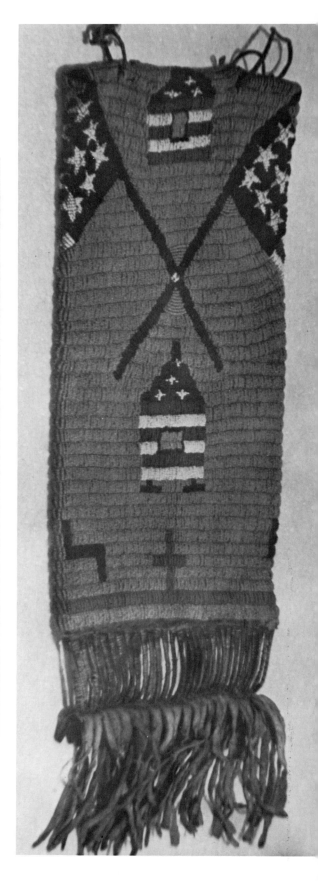

SITTING BULL'S WIFE'S BAG solid blue with the American flag and log cabin in red, white and blue. Photo by Gary VanKauwenberg. Courtesy of the Douglas County Historical Museum.

166

CLASS OF SERVICE DESIRED

DOMESTIC	FOREIGN
TELEGRAM	FULL RATE CABLE
DAY LETTER	DEFERRED CABLE
NIGHT MESSAGE	NIGHT CABLE LETTER
NIGHT LETTER	WEEK-END CABLE LETTER
SHIP RADIOGRAM	RADIOGRAM

Patrons should check class of service desired, otherwise message will be transmitted as a full-rate communication.

RECEIVER'S NUMBER

CHECK

TIME FILED

STANDARD TIME

Form 2

Send the following message, subject to the terms on back hereof, which are hereby agreed to

Superior, Wisconsin
March 31, 1934

Malcolm G. Wyer
Public Library
Denver, Colorado

    I accept your Five Hundred Dollar offer for negatives copyright included, providing you accept them in Superior and pay for them here.

                       W. K. LINK

Pho. Postal
10:30 A.M.
S.

BIBLIOGRAPHY

The following books, newspapers, collections and correspondence were consulted in preparation for this work.

I Books

1. *A Souvenir of Superior*, The Superior Evening Telegram, West Superior, Wisconsin
2. *Andreas' Historical Atlas of Dakota*, R. R. Donnelley and Sons, Lakeside Press, Chicago, 1884
3. *Barry, D.F.*, Compiled for the Superior Public Library from local newspapers. Filed by W.P.A. Project #7800 and #11068 Superior, Wisconsin, 1942.
4. *Bismarck City Directory*, R. L. Polk and Co., Bismarck, 1884
5. Burdick, Usher L., *David F. Barry's Indian Notes on "The Custer Battle"*, Wirth Brothers, Baltimore, 1949
6. *City of Superior Directory*, R. L. Polk and Co., Duluth, St. Paul and Superior, 1889-1934
7. Coffeen, Herbert, *The Teepee Book*, Sheridan, Wyoming, 1916
8. Frost, Lawrence A., *The Westerners Brand Book,* Chicago, Illinois, Volume XXI, no. 8, 1964
9. Gates, Clough, *Superior, An Outline of History*, reprinted from the Evening Telegram Centennial Edition, July 15, 1954
10. Graham, W. A., *The Custer Myth*, Bonanza Books, New York, 1953
11. *History of the City of Bismarck, North Dakota-First One-Hundred Years*, Bismarck, North Dakota, 1973
12. Holley, Frances Chamberlain, *Once Their Home*, Donohue and Henneberry, Chicago, 1890
13. Innis, Ben, *Briefly Buford*, privately published, 1963
14. *Jewell's Business and Resident Directory of Bismarck*, Bismarck, N.D., 1879
15. *Jewell's First Annual Directory of the City of Bismarck Dakota*, M. H. Jewell, Tribune Book and Job Printing House, Bismarck, D.T. 1879
16. Lass, William E., *Isaac P. Baker and the Baker Papers,* reprinted from North Dakota History, Vol. 24, No. 4, October 1957
17. *North Dakota History*, Orlando Scott Goff, Pioneer Dakota Photographer, reprinted from the Bismarck Tribune, May 12, 1949
18. *Sesquicentennial Celebration Committee Booklet*, Obrien Bros. Honeoye Falls, N.Y., 1963
19. Taft, Robert, *Photography and the American Scene*-A Social History 1839-1889 McMillan Co. New York, 1938
20. Tolman, J.C., *The Texaco Star*
21. Trinka, Zena Irma, *Out Where the West Begins,* The Pioneer Co., St. Paul, 1920
22. Walker, Judson Elliott, *Campaigns of General Custer in the Northwest and the Final Surrender of Sitting Bull*, Promontory Press, New York, 1881
23. Watson, Elmo Scott, *Orlando Scott Goff-Pioneer Dakota Photographer,* North Dakota History
24. *Wisconsin Archaeologist*, Vol. 23, No. 4

II Newspapers

1. *The Bismarck Tribune*, Oct. 15, 1873
2. Ibid. Nov. 5, 1873
3. Ibid. Nov. 15, 1873
4. Ibid. Jan. 31, 1877
5. Ibid. Feb. 21, 1877
6. Ibid. Sep. 12, 1879
7. Ibid. Jul. 30, 1880
8. Ibid. Apr. 8, 1881
9. Ibid. Apr. 15, 1881
10. Ibid. Apr. 22, 1881
11. Ibid. May 6, 1881
12. Ibid. Mar. 1883
13. Ibid. May 11, 1883
14. Ibid. Jun. 1, 1883
15. Ibid. Oct. 19, 1883
16. Ibid. May 2, 1884
17. Ibid. May 16, 1884
18. Ibid. Jun. 20, 1884
19. Ibid. Jun. 27, 1884
20. Ibid. Aug. 22, 1884
21. Ibid. Oct. 24, 1884
22. Ibid. Dec. 26, 1884
23. Ibid. Jun. 23, 1886
24. Ibid. Jun. 25, 1886
25. Ibid. Jun. 26, 1886
26. Ibid. Aug. 17, 1888
27. Ibid. Oct. 19, 1888
28. Ibid. Nov. 16, 1888
29. Ibid. Nov. 30, 1888
30. Ibid. May 11, 1890
31. Ibid. May 13, 1890
32. Ibid. May 15, 1890
33. Ibid. Jul. 13, 1909
34. Ibid. Aug. 23, 1910
35. *The Bismarck Tribune*, Mar. 19, 1926
36. Ibid. May 12, 1949
37. *The Billings Gazette*, Jun. 23, 1927
38. Ibid. Jan. 31, 1932
39. Ibid. May 8, 1932
40. *The Columbus Republican*, Columbus, Wisconsin, Sep. 15, 1933
41. *The Duluth Herald*, Mar. 6, 1934
42. *The Duluth News Tribune*, 1898
43. Ibid. Aug. 7, 1912
44. Ibid. Aug. 8, 1912
45. Ibid. Jun. 20, 1926
46. Ibid. Apr. 6, 1933
47. Ibid. Jul. 9, 1972
48. *Great Falls Tribune*
49. *The Fargo Times,* Jul. 1, 1880
50. *The Inland Ocean*, Jan. 10, 1892
51. *The Miles City Star*, Feb. 5, 1930
52. *The Minneapolis Tribune*, Feb. 24, 1888
53. *The Montana Gazette*, Jun. 29, 1926
54. *The Ray Pioneer* (Wms County, North Dakota) Sep. 15, 1932
55. *The St. Paul Pioneer Press*, Jul. 21, 1895
56. *The Sunday News Tribune*, May 20, 1888
57. Ibid. Feb. 23, 1902
58. *The Superior Daily Call*, May 15, 1890
59. Ibid. Feb. 6, 1892
60. *The Superior Evening Telegram*, May 15, 1890
61. Ibid. Dec. 15, 1894
62. Ibid. Jul. 8, 1913
63. Ibid. May 28, 1925
64. Ibid. Mar. 19, 1926
65. Ibid. Jul. 19, 1926
66. Ibid. Jul. 20, 1926
67. Ibid. Jan. 10, 1928
68. Ibid. Mar. 20, 1928
69. Ibid. May 30, 1928
70. Ibid. May 14, 1929
71. Ibid. Jul. 24, 1929
72. Ibid. Feb. 4, 1930
73. Ibid. Feb. 15, 1932
74. Ibid. Jun. 24, 1932
75. Ibid. Aug. 22, 1932
76. Ibid. Feb. 3, 1933
77. Ibid. Apr. 5, 1933
78. Ibid. Jun. 4, 1933
79. Ibid. Mar. 5, 1934
80. Ibid. Mar. 6, 1934

81. Ibid. Mar. 7, 1934
82. Ibid. Mar. 9, 1934
83. Ibid. May 4, 1944
84. *The Superior Evening Tribune*, Jan. 5, 1897
85. Ibid. Jul. 4, 1933
86. *The Superior Leader*, Sep. 6, 1891
87. *The Superior Times*, Jan. 9, 1897
88. *The Superior News Tribune,* Jan. 14, 1917
89. *The Superior Telegram*, Feb. 6, 1892
90. Ibid. Nov. 23, 1907
91. Ibid. Jul. 8, 1913
92. Ibid. Jun. 25, 1914
93. Ibid. Feb. 17, 1915
94. Ibid. Feb. 20, 1915
95. Ibid. May 1, 1915
96. Ibid. Jun. 25, 1915
97. Ibid. Nov. 1, 1916
98. Ibid. Jan. 21, 1918
99. Ibid. Sep. 28, 1920
100. Ibid. Aug. 19, 1921
101. Ibid. 1923
102. Ibid, Jun. 25, 1923
103. Ibid. Jun. 24, 1926
104. Ibid. Jun. 1-2, 1929
105. Ibid. Jul. 4, 1933
106. *The Washington Daily News*, Dec. 22, 1936
107. *The Wisconsin Sunday Times*, Jul. 24, 1921

III Collections

1. *D. F. Barry Collection*, Courtesy of the Douglas County Historical Museum, Superior, Wisconsin
2. *Elizabeth B. Custer Collection*, Courtesy of the Custer Battlefield Historical and Museum Association, Crow Agency, Montana
3. *Frank Hutchinson Collection*, Courtesy of the North Dakota Historical Society, Bismarck, North Dakota
4. *W. S. Hart County Museum*, Newhall, California
5. *D. F. Barry Collection of Photographs*, Courtesy of the Western History Dept., The Denver Public Library

IV Correspondence

1. D. F. Barry and L. W. Crawford April 9, 1922
2. D. F. Barry and General E. S. Godfrey, May 10, 1923
3. Ibid. May 3, 1926
4. D. F. Barry and Mrs. Elizabeth B. Custer, January 14, 1927
5. D. F. Barry and General E. S. Godfrey, 1928
6. D. F. Barry and Mrs. Elizabeth B. Custer, March 7, 1929
7. Ibid. March 8, 1929
8. Ibid. June 16, 1929
9. D. F. Barry and General E. S. Godfrey, Nov. 12, 1929
10. D. F. Barry and Mrs. Elizabeth B. Custer, February 4, 1931
11. D. F. Barry and Vernon Barry, April 21, 1933
12. D. F. Barry and Frank Hutchinson, January 1, 1934
13. D. F. Barry and Marlys Mae Kibbon, February 5, 1934
14. D. F. Barry and Frank Hutchinson, February 21, 1934
15. W. K. Link and M. H. Barry, March 3, 1934
16. W. K. Link and William S. Hart, March 12, 1934
17. W. K. Link and M. H. Barry, March 21, 1934
18. Ibid. March 29, 1934
19. Ibid. June 25, 1934
20. Dr. Frank C. Sarazin and M. H. Barry, January 24, 1935
21. James E. Lundsted and the New York Historical Society, October 4, 1961
22. Between the author and Mrs. Eunice Barry
23. Between the author and Mr. and Mrs. Vernon Barry
24. Between the author and Mrs. Margaret Lee, Columbus Public Library, Columbus, Wisconsin
25. Between the author and Mr. Lloyd P. Hiatt, W.S. Hart County Museum, Newhall, California
26. Between the author and Mr. John Spence and Mrs. Dorothy Malone, Honeoye Falls-Mendon Historical Society, New York
27. Between the author and Mr. John Kardon
28. Between the author and Mr. James E. Lundsted, Douglas County Historical Museum, Superior, Wisconsin
29. Between the author and Father Michael Hogan, St. Paul of the Cross Catholic Church, Honeoye Falls, New York
30. Between the author and Father Ambrose Holzer, St. Jerome's Catholic Church, Columbus, Wisconsin
31. Between the author and Mrs. Phillip G. Stratton
32. Between the author and the New York Public Library
33. Between the author and the Polish Steamship Company
34. Between the author and Lois B. Price, Portage Free Library, Portage, Wisconsin
35. Between the author and the U.S. Dept. of Commerce, Maritime Administration, Washington, D.C.
36. Between the author and Mr. Frank Vyzralek, North Dakota Historical Society
37. Between the author and the Wisconsin State Historical Society, Madison, Wisconsin

INDEX